ELITE VOICES

*Praise
for
Ericka*

"Good relationship advice encourages authenticity and vulnerability as they are essential components in building strong healthy connections. Ericka openly shares a riveting account of her dating journey (the good, bad, and ugly) and gifted us with tips, tools, and advice that would undoubtably allow her readers to flourish in dating after divorce. A must read!"

- Juanita Lomax
Founder and CEO of Hit Like A Girl
and J. Lomax Consulting Firm

"If you are going through a major life transition such as divorce, practicing self-care is of highest importance. A must read if you are looking to implement helpful self-care strategies and the shift in mindset necessary in your journey to healing and wellness."

- Dr. Paula Anderson
LCPC Organizational Psychologist/
Clinical Counselor/CEO, PACE Consulting

"As my personal development coach during a crucial season in my life, I can say with all certainty that YOU inspired and encouraged me towards becoming the woman I am meant to be! And you do it with such authenticity. "

- April Teixeira
Founder and CEO,
The Corny Bread Company, LLC

"Ericka has guided me to become my authentic self. Her empathetic listening skills, along with her expertise in conflict resolution, have been really helpful for me to learn how to shift from negative to positive responses. I am grateful to have Ericka as my coach!"

- Heather L. Carpenter, PhD

"You were magnificent at the Coke Consolidated Women's Leadership Forum. Thanks for sharing your authentic self with our audience. Your presentation was empowering on several levels!"

- Valerie Williams
Senior Manager – Engagement,
Coca-Cola Consolidated

I'm here. Now what?

Finding Joy After the Storm

I'm here. Now what?

Finding Joy After the Storm

Ericka Sallee

ELITE VOICES

ELITE VOICES
San Antonio, TX 78229

First Edition, September 2023
ISBN: 978-1-63765-404-0
Library of Congress Control Number: 2023906794

Our mission is to empower individuals and businesses to enhance their professional brand by becoming recognized experts in their field. We provide the tools and resources to help our clients become authors, establish a strong personal brand, and grow their business to achieve greater visibility, credibility, and financial success.

I dedicate this book to my children. We have shared a difficult journey, but we've weathered the storm and found new meaning in life and love. You've been two of the most amazing demonstrations of resilience and joy, and I'm blessed to be your mom. You make me laugh (sometimes harder than when I'm laughing at myself!) and you continue to be my *whys*.

Contents

Introduction

It's hard to believe it's been four years now since I wrote my first book, *Pathway to Purpose: Find It. Follow It. Fulfill It.* Truth of the matter is that I never imagined myself writing one book, let alone two. But here I am, bringing you into a new part of my world.

At the time I wrote *Pathway to Purpose*, I connected various pieces of my life that led me to a sense of knowing, of recognizing that specific events from childhood to adulthood helped me realize my calling in life. Some of those experiences were never discussed until I wrote the book. Sharing memories, some painful, was not easy, but I wanted to share my discovery with others. What I learned was that helping women move beyond hurt, pain, guilt, shame, insecurity, or whatever other negative emotion they're feeling, and showing them how to seek the best version of themselves and own their own purpose is what makes me tick. It was my hope that after you read my first book, you too would get that same sense of knowing and would be encouraged to follow your path.

At that time, I was in a choppy storm. My marriage was on the rocks, and I knew my husband and I were headed for the shore of divorce. That was a journey I didn't want to travel, but the path was becoming clearer and clearer. Divorce was imminent. In fact, I remember that as I was speaking at my *Pathway to Purpose* book signing, I was really speaking from the perspective of two worlds: the one in which I was breathing a sigh of relief that I'd finally gotten the book out of my head and into the world, and the one of impending divorce that was quite scary and had me holding my breath.

Even though I was standing in a room at Bird in Hand bookstore in Baltimore, surrounded by my closest family and friends, and sharing the inspirations, lessons, and even a few laughs from the book, I was crying on the inside. There was so much about my life that was unknown at that time. I wasn't sure how to take the first step of many that would be needed to move toward separation and divorce. No one in the room knew what I was feeling and why. But just about every person there would be affected because our divorce impacted each family member and friend who had been part of the nucleus of our marriage for so many years. Our joint families would no longer come to our house for Christmas and other celebrations. We wouldn't be showing up to other events as a couple, and our interaction with friends would change. It didn't hit me then, but as I write this, I guess you could say that day was the beginning of realization.

That was then, and now I'm in the full reality of what I was truly afraid of—divorce.

sigh

When I first started sharing with others that my husband and I were getting a divorce, and even after it was final, saying "divorce" felt as if I were uttering some kind of taboo word. I didn't want to say it, and probably whispered it when I did, as if it were top secret. There were many times when I'd ask myself what this part of my life would look like. How would I make it on my own? Could I do it? What does single even feel like? Divorced... Breathe in; breathe out. It's not a whisper now. It's a full-on word that has become easier to say and to acknowledge. There have been some difficult moments, but divorce has become easier to live with as time passes.

My guess is that if you're reading this, you're in the rough waters headed for divorce, or even in the midst of some other life transition. While the backdrop of my story is my divorce, fill in the blank for what you may be dealing with in your life. Maybe you're asking yourself the same questions, wondering how you'll make it. Perhaps you're trying to figure out how your children or family will remain whole in brokenness. But change for the better often comes in the worst of times; it's not always easy to see clearly in the moment.

Yet, going through a divorce is an opportunity for reflection, growth, and healing. You might be financially stable and have no fear of making ends meet. Or maybe you have limited income, and the thought of being the sole breadwinner terrifies you. Your identity might be so closely aligned with your spouse that you don't even recognize yourself or know what you like. If you're like me, and you're already divorced, you may be adjusting mentally, emotionally and physically while navigating the single lane and, perhaps, anticipating companionship. You might still be going through emotional growing pains as you hit every new experience where memories of the past remind you of changes in the present. Birthdays. Holidays. Kids' sporting events. Each is a reminder that celebrations and gatherings will look and feel different as a result of divorce. You might want to distance yourself, but strong support from family and friends is part of this process, whether you're feeling low or in a good place after mutually departing.

Whether you are preparing for or already divorced, I'm sure you're ready to be happy, healthy, and joyful, and to laugh, love, and have fun. This book is not intended to get you to the next right companion, though it may help you figure out what that looks like if that's your desire. It's also not to suggest that healing comes as soon as the ink on the divorce papers is dry. Rather, it's to help you connect with the very real and raw emotions that are part of the divorce experience. The intent is to aid you in channeling those emotions into the kind of energy that empowers you to move forward with your life. It's about giving you a glimmer of hope to know there is life after divorce.

This might mean discovering a new relationship with yourself and becoming clear about who you are and how you want to appear when the next right person comes along. I know there are decisions to make regarding finances, custody, child support, and all the other nuances. Of course, this can bring added stress, depending on how intertwined things are and how cooperative each party is. I'm sure you've heard stories from friends, perhaps family or couples in the news, who have gone through a divorce. Each has its own set of circumstances—some extremely painful, some shouting hallelujah, and others somewhere in between. The key is to allow yourself to feel what you need to feel and to heal the way you need to heal.

I can truly say that once I surrendered to the divorce, I was able to get through the legal logistics in the best way possible. Surrender? you ask. Yes, exactly.

First, I had to come to terms with the fact that I was getting a divorce. There was no denying growing apart, wanting different things in life, and eventually traveling down separate paths. Acknowledging this was the "letting go" part that helped nudge me—no, push me—into the deep end of the pool, so to speak. Even though I know how to swim (at least well enough to stay afloat), this was a current that I wasn't quite sure how to navigate.

Second, as difficult as it was, showing up for each mediation session meant that I was taking the steps to keep things moving. I can remember one session when my emotions were all over the place. I was a wreck. James hugged me in the parking lot after the session and said, "We're going to get through this." It was a reassuring moment I needed. We both did. It wasn't easy for either of us. In that moment, I was trying to process the emotional logistics, but wasn't quite sure how to accomplish that or how long this process would take. At some point, I learned to give myself grace with my feelings—the moments I was a wreck, the times I was at peace, and the space that was somewhere in between.

I had to come to grips with the fact that though one part of my life was ending, it was also an opportunity for a new beginning. I had a great support system in my children, family, friends, therapist, books, and even business. These are the things that made me feel loved, empowered, and purposeful. And they still do.

I don't know in what stage of divorce you are. In life, we experience things differently, and that includes divorce. Some couples don't want to interact once divorced and only tolerate each other if children are involved. Others can work through the tough moments and have an amicable relationship. Mine happened to be the latter, but the mental and emotional processing of the moving pieces was very real. I believe that as you read this book, we will connect, regardless of which end of the spectrum you're on. Perhaps through similar stories, feelings, or that spark for a new kind of happiness.

One of the biggest lessons of all is growing into healthy relationships with people who share an integral part of your life. Adjusting to how you and your ex relate to each other, with your kids, in new relationships, with other family members and friends can be awkward and uncomfortable. It will certainly feel that way in the beginning. Perhaps over a long period of time, as it did for me.

The truth is—I'm still figuring some things out. But at the end of the day, we all have a vested interest in honoring and respecting one another as we embrace this next phase of life. There are milestones to navigate, and each has its own set of emotions, some more intense than others. There were times when I didn't know how I would feel in certain situations until the moment came, and in those moments, talking to myself, relying on prayer, or leaning on trusted support was the answer. And here's one thing to make note of: It's okay not to be okay. Write that down, and plaster it in your mind.

Most importantly, I want you to know that while divorce can turn your world upside down, it doesn't have to keep you spinning. Sure, there are some messy, ugly circumstances that lead couples to end their marriage, and there can be tension throughout the process, but there is a way to get to the other side in a dignified way. It takes time, effort, and the willingness of all parties to want the best outcome. Every family gets to decide what this looks like and how to get there. For us, it meant cooperative co-parenting, respecting new relationships, and creating a culture where we can all get along in a positive way.

I also acknowledge that I am speaking from my Western-world perspective about marriage and divorce. The way I express my ideas, share my lessons, and provide insight may not align with other customs.

I won't pretend that I don't still have challenges with adapting to how my family has changed, because I do. But I celebrate areas of growth and acknowledge that I'm still a work in progress. It's my hope that you take whatever you need from my story to create your own in a way that feels good and is good for you and your family. I want the words to jump off these pages and into your heart as a reminder that you will be okay, and that it's possible to have cordial relationships after divorce. It may require time and a lot of healing along the way, but take each moment as it comes, and be kind to yourself as you go.

" I was afraid of divorce because it made me feel like a failure. "

Chapter 1

If You're Scared, Say You're Scared

I've watched enough Hallmark movies to know how the story will end. Two love interests will go through their antagonistic friction, experience the magical moment in which they discover their love, then end up living happily ever after. They're the fairy tales of modern times, but the reality is that life does not always imitate art, and people get divorced.

But I never thought that would be my story; quite frankly, I was frightened by it. I think my husband and I were both afraid of taking the next steps to end our marriage, but we knew we could no longer go on the way we were. We weren't happy. His parents were married for forty-nine years before my father-in-law passed away, and they raised three amazing children. My parents were never married, and my mom didn't marry until I was in college. Unlike my husband and some of my friends, I didn't grow up in a two-parent household. During my younger years, two of my closest cousins got married, and those were my only examples of marriage at the time.

When I got married, it was an exciting time for me and a big deal for my family and friends. My husband and I met in college, came from loving families, had decent jobs, moved into our first home, which we never dreamed we could afford, and had our first child five years after we were married. This was the definition of success for us, as it is for many people: education, job, house, and family (not necessarily in that order). Plus, we had accomplished these things in our midtwenties, which was a huge accomplishment for us. We knew plenty of people our age and older who didn't have the same experience. I think about my mom, who was raising me as a toddler when she was the same age I was when I got married. She often reflected on the difficulty of being a single mom and how happy she was that I had love and support from a partner and didn't have to raise a child on my own. I know she was proud of me and happy about the life I'd created.

I had accomplished great things early on, expanded my high school education with graduate and post-graduate degrees, and had two children. Being a divorcée felt as if it were a stain on a list of things I'd done right in my life. I was afraid of divorce because it made me feel like a failure. I knew, logically, that although my marriage had failed, *I* wasn't a failure. But negative self-talk can quickly fill up space in our heads and sound convincing. You may hear subtle, nagging whispers, such as, *See, you're divorced, so that means you're not smart!* or *What a loser!* It's silly, but when you're trying to sort things out and make sense of your life, those whispers can ring louder than a full gospel choir.

When the divorce was finalized, I still had my kids, degrees and certifications, beautiful home, career, loving family, and friends. The divorce didn't take away my accomplishments, but the negative garbage in my head was attempting to make me forget about the great things I'd done. I had to remind myself that marriage was just one thing on the list of wonderful life events that didn't work out.

I also feared the social stigma around divorce and how my family would be seen as a result. Black families are often portrayed in the media, movies, and television as dysfunctional, while White families are seen as the source of social stability. The truth of the matter is that every family, regardless of ethnicity, has moments of strife and discord, no matter what the social narrative is. But I silently wondered how this was going to play out for us, especially since we lived in a small, predominantly White town. Our children had been involved in recreational and sports activities with the same families for years, so people were used to seeing us at various activities—shopping, attending school and sports events, entering dance competitions, dining out, and interacting in the neighborhood.

Then there is the myth that Black fathers are not present in the lives of their children. While this is true for some, it's certainly not so for all. Deadbeat dads and moms come from all walks of life.

I didn't want our divorce to be a misguided representation of either of these perceptions. It was important to us to do our best to adapt to our new normal and create stability for our children. My ex-husband is very much a part of our children's lives. He's present and available to both, so it doesn't matter what the perception is. That's not our story, and I'm grateful for this.

I realize this is not true for everyone. If your situation is different from mine, the most important thing is to ensure that your children feel loved and supported by your presence. Engage a supporting cast of family and friends who can be a part of your circle as much as possible. Though it may not be easy, try your best not to bad-mouth your ex, at least not in front of the kids!

My fear was more about what other people would think versus the reality of what we were doing to get through that difficult time. So there was no real basis for my fear, and now I don't spend a lot of time wondering what other people think. If, by chance, you've been fearful of what people may be thinking about your life and family, remember it's *your* life and *your* family. No one but you and your spouse can make decisions in your best interest.

I encourage you to include your children in the process, especially if they are old enough to understand what is happening with their parents. One of my biggest regrets is that we did not communicate as often as we should have with our kids about what steps we were taking with the marriage. We prolonged telling them that we were separating because, quite frankly, we dreaded it and didn't know how to approach it. When we finally sat down to tell them that we were separating, it hurt me to my core. My son was openly tearful, and my daughter was quiet and reserved, though I know they were feeling the same hurt. I replayed those images of their reactions in my mind for quite a while, and every time I did, it broke my heart. From that point on, I think we may have been subconsciously trying to shield them from more of that hurt by keeping the separation logistics away from them.

After we announced our separation to the kids, James and I remained in the house together, cordially managing the day-to-day routine, but the elephant was in every room. Sometimes, I'd sleep in the spare bedroom; most times, we'd eat dinner together; and, oftentimes, we'd go our separate ways for family functions. We continued this for months, but knew it wasn't sustainable. We started looking at mediation options, and then went to the sessions and did things behind the scenes to end our marriage, but we never told the kids about any of it.

One day, I casually mentioned to my daughter that we were working through the custody arrangement, and she said, "Wait, I didn't know you guys were even going through mediation!"

I still blew it off because there was "no need for them to worry; we are taking care of everything."

The next milestone came when we sat down to tell the kids their dad was moving out. My daughter was away at school, so we broke the news over a FaceTime call, while James and I sat in the family room with our son. We did the best we could with that conversation, trying to assure our children that we loved them and that we would get through everything together. It was a solemn moment, and I remember wishing my daughter were physically with us, instead of dealing with the news alone. It was approximately a year between the time we first told them we were separating and when we told them Dad was moving out. During that time, we had been living some sense of normalcy that we all knew was not normal at all. By the time their dad moved out, it was as if a wound had opened back up before it was completely healed.

As I reflect, I know for sure that it was completely selfish of us to exclude our children from some of the basic details of the mediation process. Our attempt to spare their emotions wasn't making it easier for them. It was allowing us, their parents, to delay addressing and witnessing a huge part of the reality we were facing—the impact of the divorce on our kids. They later confirmed our bad decision-making by politely informing me—and I'm sure they shared the same with their dad—that we did not give them enough credit for being able to handle the situation. They were right.

Though I cannot go back to change the way we communicated in our situation, it is my hope that as you read this, it will help you to share more with your kids if you're just starting the separation process. Their ages will determine how to have that conversation, but children are more resilient than we think, especially with the right guidance and approach about divorce. And if you're just as frightened and uncertain as I was about how to have the conversation, check out this article—"Children and Divorce," published by HelpGuide.org I found while writing this book. There is a wealth of information in it that I wish I'd discovered while going through our process. But it's a great reference for you…in addition to this book, of course!

Yes, divorce hurts, and it is not easy. But if the kids see Mom and Dad working together in the best way possible while loving them through it, they will be okay.

I'd never lived on my own, and the thought of doing it for the first time in my fifties was a little daunting. When I graduated from college, I moved back home with my mom and stepdad. James and I were dating at the time, and after six months, we moved into our first apartment, got engaged, married, and then moved into our first home. The next twenty-five-plus years became a part of our history. In that span of time, we were a two-income household, and I never paid a bill on my own, so to think about doing it by myself was enough to make me nervous. Hell YES, I was afraid! Managing and maintaining the household would be on me—mortgage, groceries, utilities, car, insurance, broken this, and malfunctioning that. Could I manage all of it as the sole provider, especially when we had our struggles with two incomes? This was a question silently running through my mind, while I continued to declare outwardly, ignoring fear, that I could.

I remember the first time the light bulb went out in the garage. I immediately thought, *How in the hell am I going to get up there to change it?* I was literally standing in the middle of the garage, looking up at the light as if the longer I stood there, it would magically change itself. Then it hit me. This was one of the things that James always did. I never watched or asked any questions because I knew he'd take care of it. It was just one of the roles we seemed to slip into as a married couple. He did the ladder stuff, anything that required the toolbox, and took care of the grass, to name a few. I cooked (mostly), coordinated holiday dinners and family vacations. Looking back, I probably should have paid more attention to the screws and drill bits!

For a minute, I stood in the garage, half frozen, trying to figure out how to change that damn bulb and feeling a little sad too. It was a subtle reality check that this was now my responsibility. I looked around the garage and spotted the ladder, which may as well have been an alien because that, too, was something he'd always used. Even when he set it up for me to swap out decorations in the high window over our front door, he was there to spot me. How was I supposed to open that ladder? I had to get it done.

Then I realized my son was in the house. I called for him to come help so we could figure it out together. I'd either send him up the ladder and spot him, or vice versa. I decided to climb up and change the bulb because if I needed to do it again during a time when my son was with his dad, I wanted to be prepared. Plus, he learned how to do it too. At first, it was as if we were two people trying to put together a thousand-piece puzzle after dumping all the pieces on the floor. We stared at the ladder, started pulling the knobs, and shifted it around a few times, but we finally figured it out. Once the light bulb was changed and the ladder put away, I enjoyed the victory of getting it done. Who knew such a small thing would come with such an immense sense of pride and accomplishment.

There were many other light-bulb moments, similar to the old shed in the backyard that was literally on its last leg. The fact that a strong wind hadn't blown it down years before our divorce was a sheer miracle. When I changed homeowner's policies, a representative from the new company came to do a home inspection. I was immediately told that, before they could write the new policy, the shed had to be torn down because it was in such bad condition it was a liability. Uh-oh. I had no clue who to reach out to for the demolition or how much it would cost. Thankfully, the insurance agent recommended a handyman, so I called him; he gave me a reasonable price and told me when he could come tear down the shed. Thank God!

When you're married, you can divide and concur when things need to be done around the house. Maybe one person does the research to find the fixer-uppers, and the other person allocates the financial resources to take care of the matter. As a single homeowner, the problem-solving for expected and unexpected things that come up with the house, car, or other maintenance rests squarely on you. This is enough to fill your mind with fear when managing by yourself, but here are some things that have helped me get through those moments:

1. Ask for help. We're not superhuman, and no one can do everything by themselves. Besides, contrary to a misguided narrative, asking for help is not a sign of weakness. It's a sign of strength.

2. Barter. Think about what you can give in exchange for the assistance you require. The same handyman who tore down my shed also hauled away my old office furniture. He was able to use one of the cabinets and an old microwave, which made his fee reasonable.

3. Ask for a payment arrangement. This is always an option. You may not have thousands of dollars in reserve. Arranging to break the payment for a large ticket item into smaller, more manageable payments over time can be a good solution.

Of course, if you're leasing your home after divorce, it's much easier and less costly for you to call the landlord or submit a repair order.

Thankfully, I've been able to make it work. The very first year I began managing the household on my own was in 2020, during the pandemic. My income and business were steady, allowing me to pay my expenses, buy food, and even travel a bit when it was safe enough to do so. Don't get me wrong. There were times when it was a little tight, but God always made a way, whether I received a new client, had to shift things around in the budget to make it work, or roll coins to get through a rough patch. Yes, I did that. Those were truly faith moments and reminders that I was not walking this journey alone.

Another reality check came the day James moved out. We had already agreed on what he would take from the house and when he would move—during a time when our son and I were out of the house. We didn't want our son to see that part of the process; our daughter was away at school, so she wouldn't witness it. We were trying to lessen the emotional strain wherever we could. On the list of items that would go with my husband was our living room furniture, which had followed us from our first house. I have pictures of family sitting on that same furniture in our first house the day of our daughter's christening. Smiling, happy, joyful. That same furniture was covered with our daughter's belongings as we were preparing to ship her off to college. What a bittersweet moment.

On the way back home that day, I mentioned to my son and niece that "Dad was taking the living room furniture to his new place." They had little to say, and I tried to play it cool when we walked into the house and saw the empty space. It was an undeniably strange feeling for all of us. We didn't say much, but we didn't need to...at least I didn't think so. Now I wonder if I missed another opportunity to have a conversation about how we were feeling in the moment, or even a conversation James and I should have had with our son before that day. The reality is that we did what we thought was best.

In the days that followed, when I was in the house alone, it really hit me. I stood in the middle of the living room. An empty space. I felt empty too. That space had been occupied with the same set of furniture for years, and it held so many memories. Now it was gone, and I had to figure out how to move on without it, not just the furniture but my life as I knew it.

I walked by that empty room every day for about a week or so. A couple of times, I tried to quickly move by and not look in there, even though it's one of the first rooms I see when I walk up and down the stairs. It was hard. Then, one day, I decided to go stand in the space again. It still felt strange, but this time, instead of staying quiet and reflecting on my fear, I spoke out loud and said, "This room is empty, and now I get to fill it with something new."

That moment is still vivid in my mind. This wasn't just about the furniture; it was the next step in my lifestyle change. Everything was changing, from identifying myself as divorced on documents and in conversations, to using both sinks in the bathroom and all the closet space in the bedroom. These were simple things, but reminders that it was a whole new world.

Due to COVID, our daughter came home from college in March of 2020 to finish her semester virtually. That was the most challenging time for everyone in the world. Saying this still blows my mind because of how true it is. Being in quarantine was such a mental, physical, and emotional strain on all of us. Like others, we had to figure out how to get through COVID and the divorce at the same time. Talk about a double whammy.

A few months after my daughter came home, I began giving our home a face-lift. The kids were such a huge help in the process. Purging, painting, and buying new furniture became our pastime, and words can't explain how delighted I was to fill that empty living room space with a fresh, new look. The home improvements kept us occupied during the pandemic, but it was also cathartic and healing because it gave us a chance to create new life in our home. We all needed to feel joy and excitement during a time when we were struggling to process so much at one time. It was a reset, yes, but it was still an adjustment because as we were changing the rooms, we were reminded that there were three of us, instead of four.

On the night after I wrote this chapter, I went to sit in the living room, as I'd done so many times before. This time was different. I was reflective as I sat looking around the room. I don't recall where the kids were, but the house was quiet. It was as if I were in a movie with scenes of our lives flashing rapidly before me. There was an overwhelming feeling that washed over me. The tears fell then, too, as they did the first time I stood in the room when it was empty. Only, this time, they were joyful tears. There was an extreme sense of gratitude, not just because the room was filled again, and I was able to pay for the furniture with cash, but because God got me to this point. Just as before, this moment wasn't about the furniture that now occupied the space. It was about stepping into something new. I was still unsure of many things, but I had gotten to this point, and I couldn't let the moment pass without taking the time to let that sink in. There's no doubt in my mind. My faith had been more dominant than the fear.

I also realize that some people may be fearful of divorce due to faith considerations. If you got married in the church, as we did, then you professed your vows before God, friends, and family. Many churches and cultures view divorce as the ultimate sin, one totally unacceptable to God. Though we married in the church, we had not held on to this view so stringently that we would have stayed in an unhappy marriage for the sake of the church. This doesn't mean we did not pray for God to restore our marriage. We did. But we had to look at our situation from a broader perspective.

Perhaps, this will be something you have to consider. I believe that God honors and highly favors marriage. However, I also believe that He intends for us to be happy and joyful and to feel a sense of wholeness. Unhappiness can rob us of all this. Staying in a marriage that is unhappy can be emotionally toxic and physically draining; it can keep us from living the best life God intends for us. No matter what title you give your spirit guide, or even if you don't refer to one at all, ponder whether you're supposed to go through this life miserably or merrily.

As you and your spouse make the decisions for your family—and if you know you've done everything you can to make it work, but to no avail—take the next best step. If divorce is the solution for your happiness and a better quality of life, pursue that. Then rely on your higher source to see you through, whether that be God, Allah, Buddha, friends, or family.

If you are going through a divorce, you may be experiencing some fear along with many other emotions. I totally get it. Acknowledge what you feel; you're human. Then work through the fears to figure out what's real and rational. For instance, you may be afraid that you won't be able to manage your schedule and all your kids' activities during the weeks when they're in your care. And maybe you're the person who's not used to asking for help, so the fear intensifies, and your stress is heightened. You can put the fear in check by talking to other parents who may be able to cover carpools.

There were quite a few times that I had to enlist the help of other parents to give my son a ride to or from various activities on my custody weeks. At first, that negative voice crept into my head, telling me that I was not a good parent if I couldn't transport my own child. In those moments, I had to resort back to the mantra "It's okay to ask for help." Besides, when other parents know that you're going through a divorce, many will offer to help anyway; this is another reminder of how silly our negative thoughts sound and how irrational they can be.

More time has passed, and I have to say that those initial fears have lessened. I take one day at a time, one situation at a time. And as they come, I figure out if it's something I can handle on my own or if I need the help of others. It helps me to keep things in perspective and maintain my sanity at the same time. Above all, I know my spiritual foundation is what sustains me.

This is certainly not your typical Hallmark movie. It's my story, and it's still evolving.

" I realized the awakening of faith that I was stirring up. "

Chapter 2

The Awakening

It's one thing to make the decision to get a divorce. It's quite another to get the ball rolling, and that was intimidating for me. The thought of using a lawyer felt as if it were a mountain James and I weren't sure how to climb, not to mention the unknown legal fees. I called a few lawyers who had been recommended to me and inquired about making an appointment. Then contemplated for a while about what to do next and with which of the lawyers I'd schedule time. I finally made an appointment with one whose name I can't recall, but I do remember how I felt during that initial inquiry.

Her tone was friendly, and she didn't rush through the call, which definitely reduced my stress in the moment. And the initial consultation was free! It's the little things that help us feel okay when we're navigating tough times.

On the day of my appointment, I felt strange from the moment I left the house to the time I sat at the table across from the female lawyer. All the names recommended to me were female. I was thinking of the solidarity, understanding, and compassion that a female lawyer would show a female client. Logical, right? When I got there, I wasn't sure what questions to ask other than, "How much will this cost me?"

The office was comfortable, warm, and inviting. The desk where we sat was big, but not so large that I felt disconnected. She was pleasant, asked me questions, and told me about Maryland law and all the things we would need to take into consideration, like custody and child support. I took notes while feeling nervous and nauseous. There was so much to process. That was the first time that I was front and center with all the legal wranglings associated with ending a marriage. At first, the divorce felt conceptual, but that appointment made it more concrete.

I believe she could sense that I had gotten enough information for the moment because she said something similar to, "Go home, and think it over."

I thanked her for her time, walked to my car, and cried on the way home. *Now what?*

About a month or so passed before I decided to call the lawyer's office to inquire about a follow-up meeting. Processing the information from the first meeting was overwhelming, so I was in no hurry to call back. When I did, I was nicely told the hourly rate and that the lawyer I initially met with had retired.

I had avoided making the initial contact and waited for what felt as if it were an eternity before following up. The thought of having to reengage with someone new caused me to crawl into a shell. I politely said I'd think it over. I never called back.

Looking back, I realize this was no coincidence. I believe it was a sign to let me know that wasn't the best path forward. I don't want this to seem as if I have something against lawyers. I know there are many professionals who work well to do right by their clients in a collaborative and healthy way.

I didn't mention to James that I'd even spoken to a lawyer. Maybe I was in denial, avoiding the issue, or perhaps I didn't want him to think I was striking first. That comment sounds silly, but I think this was part of the mentality I had about getting a lawyer in the first place. The notion that this would be some sort of knock-down, drag-out fight was something we both wanted to avoid because that wasn't the way our relationship had ever been, and we didn't want to start then. Plus, we were still living in the same house and doing the best we could to effectively manage our family under the circumstances.

Around that time, I was having a conversation with a dear friend who was going through her divorce around the same time. She mentioned how she, her husband, and their lawyers were in a hearing, and her husband was talking in a way that was uncharacteristic of him. My friend's thought was that it was her husband's voice speaking, but he was using the words that his lawyers were prompting him to say. As it turned out, those words were untrue and hurtful, and really could have been even more detrimental to their outcome. She described how bitter and raw the proceedings were, which made the process even more difficult. My husband and I didn't want that kind of struggle. The divorce process was difficult enough without extra drama.

Thankfully for us, we had a family member who had just gone through a separation, and they shared their experience of using a mediator. I was sorry that others we loved were going through the same situation, but appreciated that they presented us with the option. I was relieved when James came home one day and suggested that we consider a mediator. Using one had never crossed my mind. I'm not sure why, especially since I have a master's degree in negotiation and conflict management. I had an entire class on mediation *and had* saved my highlighted, dog-eared textbooks. But I suppose when it came to my own conflict, amnesia seemed to set in, and I couldn't care less about those classes. You may know exactly how that feels. You can help everybody else around you figure out their problems and be the ear they need, but at wits' end navigating your own troubles. And all the degrees in the world don't stop you from being human.

Our family member told us that mediation would be an easier and less costly way to go, which certainly piqued my interest, considering the hourly rate I'd received from the lawyer with whom I'd consulted. But there was still the dilemma of where to start. We decided that each of us would research mediators, come up with a list, and then sit down to compare. I did a Google search, looked for mediators close to where we lived, and contacted my therapist for recommendations. My husband and I sat down to compare notes. Oddly enough, there was one practice that both of us had on our list. We considered this a good sign, so that's where we started.

We called to make an appointment with the mediator. On the day of the appointment, James and I arrived separately, but at the same time. We walked up to the door, and he cordially held it for me, as he had done so many times before. Almost as if we were going out to dinner—but this was no dinner.

The mediator made the first meeting as honest, sincere, and comfortable as possible. His office was small but quaint; his desk, also small. My husband and I sat across from each other, the mediator in the middle. I know how important spacing is in a room to minimize the power dynamic. A large room and table in a bigger space may feel as if you were so far apart that reaching a mutual agreement would be difficult. A smaller space is intimate and more conducive to collaboration. So I know the setup was an intentional part of the mediation process, and I have to say it worked. When we sat at the table in that environment, it felt calm and nonthreatening. I can't help but wonder how it would have felt sitting in the lawyer's office—she and I on one side of the table, my husband and his lawyer on the other. I'm sure it would have been a totally different experience.

The divorce process was carefully explained to us, including all the areas we'd have to address to reach a separation agreement: parenting (how we would coordinate schedules and effectively co-parent), child support (how financial support for the kids would be handled), and financial arrangements (settling assets and debts). The mediator gave us his fee schedule and a written document outlining our agreement to work with him. The fee was something we could manage, and at first glance, the agreement seemed simple. He encouraged us to take it home, review it, make notes of any questions we had, and we'd discuss them in the next session.

We did just that. It was a relief to see the agreement was easy to read and comprehend. I would have been extremely frustrated if it was filled with a bunch of complex legal jargon. We agreed to move ahead with the mediation services because it lowered our cost, compressed the time to get to a legal separation agreement, and helped buffer some of the other legal aspects that may have added unnecessary complexity for what we needed. All this allowed us to move on more quickly. It wasn't easy once the sessions started, yet I hadn't expected it to be. In some sessions, I was okay. In others, I felt dazed and quite emotional. At first, I was trying to be strong, not wanting to cry. But, hell, my marriage was over, and that hurt. So, yes, I was sad, and after a while, I stopped trying to hold back the tears. Since the mediator always kept a box of tissues on the table, I used them whenever I needed.

Remember to give yourself time to feel your emotions. Suppressing our feelings about the loss is not healthy, and when we hold back, those emotions can explode in many different directions. We may find ourselves short-tempered with our children, disconnected from family, ineffective in our work, neglectful of ourselves, and emotionally unavailable for the next person. Go ahead and cry, the ugly cry if you have to; it's important that you release your emotions.

There are two sessions that I remember vividly. One was narrowing down parenting details and how we'd share custody. Our daughter was in her late teens, so parenting and child support were mainly for our son since he was still a minor. We were discussing how to share the time we spent with the children. The mediator suggested a schedule with which we didn't agree, and we made it clear that we wanted some flexibility. School, sports, work, and life in general would require us to make adjustments. We all agreed to this and made sure that flexibility was documented in the agreement.

As you go through your process, know that you and your spouse have the final say in what will work best for you. The mediator—or lawyer, if you choose—is there to guide, not dictate.

Once we agreed on the schedule, my mind immediately shifted to an image of my son going to and from our house and his dad's with a suitcase. For some reason, that picture in my head really bothered me. I don't know if it was because I thought he'd be sad during the transfer or because I cried every time he left. Maybe a combination of the two. Perhaps I'd watched too many movies and allowed fictional moments to be planted in my mind as reality. I had no idea how that experience would go, so I'd created a scenario in my head to match the emotions with which I was struggling.

My recommendation is to take a different approach than I did. Instead of trying to figure out all the *hows* while you go through the legal paperwork, try to focus on the *whats*. *What* is the parenting arrangement? *What* needs to be done with the house, cars, etc.? Take the list of *whats* home and set it on a table for a day or so. This may give your mind a chance to slow down, reset, and open the mental space you'll need to think about options. Then make the time for you and your spouse to work on the *hows* in a rational way. Trying to process the *whats* and *hows* at the same time may be too overwhelming and cause a delay in coming up with a reasonable plan.

By the way, we created a system that works when it's time to transport our son between houses. We check in with our son to see how he feels about carrying his things to and from. He seems to be fine with it. But, yes, I cried the first time he went to his dad's. Okay, okay...the second, third, and fourth times too, but it has gotten easier. His dad and I check in with him periodically to make sure he's still okay with the arrangements we've made.

The second session that I clearly recall was on finances. I'm grateful that we did not have any credit-card debt or lots of other financial ties that could have been messy and complicated. Our house was the biggest asset and connection we had, other than our children. The house we'd raised our family in for twelve years was at the center of the discussion.

On more than one occasion, James suggested we sell the house, but I was always reluctant. At first, it was because the thought of selling it was a sure sign that our marriage was ending; every time we had those conversations, I was riddled with sadness. Then, I later realized that my hesitancy was about something deeper.

It might sound crazy, but moving our children to someplace new was the last thing I wanted to do. See, I was raised by a wonderful single mom who did the best she could for me and my sister, when she came along ten years later. But there were times when we struggled to make ends meet. Part of that struggle was that we moved seven times from the time I was nine years old until I got married at the age of twenty-four. It was just how things were for us, and along with that came an instability that I wanted to prevent my children from experiencing.

I told the mediator that I wanted to keep the house and that it was something James and I had talked about multiple times. Once James realized I was adamant about keeping the house, he didn't put up much of a fight.

During the session, the mediator asked, "So you'll be able to pay the mortgage on your own?"

And I immediately responded, "Yes."

Though I spoke the word "yes" with confidence, I had a knot and butterflies in my stomach; it was fluttering so furiously I felt as if I were going to throw up. We were in the final stages of the separation agreement, and this was the last issue to resolve. I may have sounded confident in my quick response, but the pang of fear was gnawing at my insides. After all, we were saying that I would pay the mortgage by myself, something I'd never done before. There were times when it was tight for us to pay the mortgage with two incomes. A million thoughts were running through my head, and every word spoken in the room from that point on may as well have been "blah, blah, blah." All I could really hear was my own voice saying yes. I realized the awakening of faith that I was stirring up at the same time. I'd certainly need all the faith I could muster to get me through this experience and to manage everything on my own.

It took us about five months to get a final separation agreement finalized. I believe I cried during or after every session, and I often felt sad and weary. It was tough on James, too, but I have to admit that we both breathed a sigh of relief when mediation was over. One step toward the finish line.

After the separation agreement was signed, I was able to refinance the house in my name, which was a huge first step toward my independence. The time of this writing marks the third year that I've been paying the mortgage on my own, on time, every month. Remember that faith I said I needed? God has been meeting me every step of the way, and even when I needed to shift priorities during lean budget times, His grace was sufficient.

I recognize that every situation is different, so my solution may not work for you, or it just might be the perfect fit to help you dissolve your marriage. Assess the things you have to settle, think about how amicable you two will be through the process, and consider the pros and cons of using a mediator versus a lawyer; then make the decision that's in the best interest of you and your family.

" The only thing we could do was cherish each other, take one day at a time, and do our best to create a new way of being. **"**

Chapter
3

Family Ties

I met James in college. When we had a chance to talk, I told him that he looked exactly like a guy from my high school. When I mentioned my high school friend's name, James said, "Oh, that's my cousin!" At first, I thought he was just putting me on to keep the conversation going, but I later discovered that they were indeed related. We laughed at the irony of the connection, but that was the first of many to come. As we grew closer and our families started interacting, we discovered my dad and uncle went to the same high school as James's uncle, which happened to be the rival school to mine. So we had lots of fun trash-talking every chance we got.

I went to the same middle school as my oldest sister-in-law, Jessica, though we never mentioned the word "in-law" whenever we spoke of one another. We weren't in the same friend circle in school, but we could relate to some of the same stories and people. My other sister-in-law, Camille, my sister, Toshah, and I had a unique bond. We often reflected on how Camille and Toshah were so much alike, and Jessica and I were similar in our ways. Whenever we planned family gatherings, Jessica and I organized games, place settings, decorations, and coordinating colors; Camille and Toshah volunteered to bring cups and plates, but they weren't guaranteed to match! Oh, how they'd give us the blues after all our meticulous planning!

Jessica and I coordinated a number of summer trips to the beach with our kids, and we looked forward to sharing that time every year. We had our share of great memories on those trips, from planning the food beforehand, to the way we screamed with excitement when we all arrived at the lodging spot, and all the fun in between.

My mother-in-law, stepmom, and a host of family and friends were educators, so that was a common bond for them. There were many things that made the two families feel like one big family, even before James and I got married. It's often been said that when two people marry, their families join together too. I firmly believe this, and it may be a disaster for some if the families don't get along. For others, it's a wonderful bond, as was the case for James and me. We had such a unique blend with his side of the family, my mom and stepdad, my dad and stepmom, cousins, and close friends from both families. When his family hosted something, my mom and dad's sides of the family were always invited, and vice versa. When we gathered, there was always good food, laughter, and fun. Summer cookouts, vacations, holiday gatherings, football parties, "just because" hangouts, birthdays, and special occasions were moments to which we all looked forward. One of my fondest memories was a massive family cookout every summer. The backyard was a symbol of just how intertwined we were. It was a melting pot of both sides of the family, with all the food and even a specialty drink that everyone enjoyed. Those were good times.

When James and I divorced, the change in our immediate family circle was difficult, but it was just as hard coming to grips with the fact that the connection between our extended families would also change. This was not an easy adjustment to make and is a work in progress to this day. It has been awkward for me to try to figure out how I fit into James's family post-divorce, after I'd been a part of it for a good portion of my adult life.

One of the turning points was the first Christmas Eve after James moved out of the house. It was the first holiday that was different than our traditional hosting of Christmas dinner for both families. Every year before the separation, I prepared dinner, James made the oatmeal cookies, and my daughter the chocolate chip. After we separated, we agreed that he'd come to the house on Christmas Eve, make the cookies, hang out, and spend Christmas Day with the kids and me. We wanted to do our best to have some sort of normalcy during the holidays.

My sister Jessica did too; she had the brilliant idea of also coming to the house on Christmas Eve with my mother-in-law, sister, and my nieces to hang out with wine, snacks, Christmas music, and our usual silly banter. We had a wonderful time, and there was so much about that night that reminded us of all the other good times we'd had, but we all knew that so much was changing. When the night was over the extra-tight hugs and "I love yous" were heartfelt; they made me happy and sad at the same time. This was my family, and I loved them dearly, but the fact of the matter was that I really didn't know what our relationship would look like in the future. I decided to take in the moment and release myself from trying to figure anything else out that night.

The second turning point came the very next day, Christmas Day. It wasn't the house full of guests, eating, drinking, and opening gifts with wrapping paper all over the family room floor. James and I were always great hosts, making sure everything in the house was festive and fun, including decorations, music, and food. But that Christmas was rather quiet and subdued with just my mom, stepdad, sister, niece, the kids, and their dad. It was just a different atmosphere; I could sense that we all felt it, but we just went along with the day. I know our kids were glad that we kept a portion of the tradition intact, especially since our separation was still very fresh. It was pleasant, but I certainly felt the heaviness of knowing we had spent our last Christmas together as the family unit to which we were accustomed.

After Christmas, I was somewhat withdrawn because I knew my place with my in-laws had changed. I felt more and more like an outsider, and it wasn't because they'd done anything to make me feel that way. In fact, my mother-in-law and sisters had reminded me on numerous occasions how much they loved me; of course, I'm the mother to their grandchildren, niece, and nephew, so that connection would always remain. And *they* will always have a special place in my heart.

That feeling of distance was just one of the aftereffects of divorce. Once James started a new relationship, the gap between his family and me felt even wider. It was just the nature of how our lives were changing. While on one of the beach vacations with Jessica and our kids, I shared my feelings with her about how awkward I felt, for the first time ever, not fitting in with the family. The conversation went from shock that I'd feel that way, to supporting one another because, after all, my in-laws were adjusting too. The separation was a huge change for *everybody*, not just for me. No, things weren't as they used to be, so the only thing we could do was cherish each other, take one day at a time, and do our best to create a new way of being.

Maybe you're trying to come to grips with the same feelings I had about the change in your extended family. It's not easy, by any means, especially if your family was as interconnected as ours. You may find yourself having the nostalgic "remember when" conversations when you're telling stories about things that have happened over the years, or while looking at pictures from family gatherings.

Even while writing this chapter, I had a few teary-eyed moments when thinking about those memories and realizing how much things have changed. I allow myself to have those moments because family ties run deep for a long time. But I appreciate the fact that, even though we may not spend holidays or as many special occasions together, we still connect with phone calls or texts and see each other when we can. It's our new normal.

It may take time to discover what your new family norm looks like. Talk to each other, share how you feel, and figure out what's comfortable and reasonable for those most impacted. If your bond was not close, then the separation of families may be a welcome relief. I have some family members who are divorced, and they have absolutely nothing to do with their exes or families. The fact that there were no children involved in those divorces made the break easier, and that's okay.

As old family ties change, new ones may also develop. Be prepared for your ex to find someone new; there's a real possibility it will happen before you begin a new relationship. This means there's a new family dynamic that may require the same level of mental and emotional navigation as the divorce itself.

This was the case for me. I recall a session in which our mediator mentioned that we'd have to think about how to introduce our kids to someone new when either of us started dating. I didn't think much of it during that session. In fact, when I heard him mention it, I think it went in one ear and out the other; I never really thought about what that would be like. But when that time came and James started seeing someone, it was awkward, uncomfortable, and, yes, difficult. It wasn't easy for me, knowing he'd moved on, nor for my kids because they had to get used to their dad being with someone who wasn't their mother.

The reality is that it was tough for James and his new companion, Michelle, as well. We were all trying to operate in new territory for which there was no playbook; at least, we didn't have one. There were lots of conversations—my kids and their dad, James and I, and even Michelle and I. Yes, you read that right!

We were preparing for our daughter's going-away party. She had just graduated from college and was getting ready to start her new life and career in Atlanta. It was such a happy time for our family because we were all so proud of her. It was also a stressful time because part of the planning included making up the guest list of family and friends who would attend her party, which I was hosting at my house.

One day, we were sitting on the deck when my daughter asked if it would be okay for her to invite Michelle to the party. I had been expecting the question, but I still wasn't quite prepared, and I honestly didn't want to answer right then. I needed some time to think about it. I didn't want to rush my healing and dealing with my emotions; they were still pretty raw at that time. I had to get through this new stage at my own pace, so surely the answer had to be no. I wasn't quite ready to have my soon-to-be ex, his new girlfriend, and both sides of our family in my house to celebrate our daughter. I'm sure it was an uneasy time for James and Michelle too.

My daughter was kind about how I was feeling, and I know that she had to get to her own place of healing to even ask if Michelle could attend. It weighed on me for a bit, but I didn't have a lot of time to wrestle with the answer because the party was about a week away. I also had a conversation with my sister, Toshah, who understood how uneasy I felt, but assured me that she'd support whatever decision I made. This was a reminder of how important it is to have people who can hold you up when you need it most.

I had to make a decision, and I wanted to do the right thing. I didn't think I was ready, but I said yes. Even after I did so, I second-guessed myself. *Did I make the best decision? What is the family going to think? How will they respond? Do I really want* her *in my house? The house that we'd shared as a family?* Then I had to stop myself. This party wasn't about me; it was about our daughter. And the reality was that James and Michelle were an instrumental part of this major event in our daughter's life. They'd supported her and purchased some of the things she needed for the move.

A new partner who cares for your kids is of utmost importance, and it was clear that Michelle was embracing them in a loving way. And as difficult as it had been for our daughter to adjust to our new life, she was grateful for their support; I was too. Besides, both of our kids were trying to heal and do their best to get to a better place in the new family dynamic.

I realized that all the questions I was asking myself to make me doubt my decision were getting in the way of a pivotal opportunity for the start of my own healing. Did it come sooner than I'd planned? Absolutely. But I could either kick and scream, or I could put my big-girl panties on and lean into the moment.

Michelle and I agreed to speak before the party because it made sense for us to clear the air and minimize any awkwardness that might arise from seeing each other for the first time in a family setting. Leading up to that first conversation with her, I felt a mix of nervous energy and anticipation. I wasn't sure who would speak first or how long the conversation would last, and it was hard to refrain from analyzing how the call would go before it happened, which created more angst. During the call, I was actually pretty relaxed, and the conversation itself was too. We talked as two adult women, free of contention, and focused on the fact that this was a first step in the process of moving on. The call didn't last long; afterward, I felt relieved, and I'm sure she did too.

Once that conversation was over, I made a few calls to my family to let them know that Michelle would be attending the party. I didn't want anyone to be surprised, and I wanted to have the right energy in the house for the celebration. And as strange as it may seem, I later thought about how Michelle must have felt. She was walking into a situation that was just as uncomfortable for her, so I'm sure she had to process her own feelings about being around my family as the new person in James's life.

As I was getting dressed on the day of the party, I thought about what would happen in that first moment when the two of them arrive. *Do we just wave? Hug? Shake hands?* But when they got to the house, we cordially greeted each other with a smile and hellos, and I welcomed them into the house. It was similar to getting into a pool on a hot day. You know the water is going to be cool, but you're not sure how cold. First, you dip your toe in, and then you slowly ease the rest of your body into the water. After realizing that the water is actually refreshing, you release your apprehension and become free to enjoy it. That's how the party turned out.

Everyone seemed to enjoy themselves. There were times when Michelle and I were in close proximity, making small talk and exchanging pleasantries. The house was filled with people moving about inside and out, so we had ample space around us. It was the first time both sides of the family had been together since our separation, and it literally felt like old times. Good food, drinks, and lots of laughter created the best party vibe. That was all that mattered.

While that party went well and everyone got along, there were later celebrations in which I wasn't quite ready to embrace all of us being together. Maybe it was petty. Maybe I was reverting back to transitioning at my own pace. After all, we had a good experience at our daughter's party, so why not just keep it going for other combined gatherings? All I can say is I was on a roller coaster and still processing a lot of my emotions after the loss that comes with divorce. One moment, you're okay and feeling as if you're moving on well. The next minute, you're not okay and feeling stuck in your feelings.

Moving on takes time. There are good days and bad days, and that's okay. Be kind to yourself when you experience those moments.

Since then, more has changed, and we continue to move forward. There have been family events, soccer and football games, and school dances for our son that we've all shared. Yes, I felt a little awkward at the first few soccer games we all attended. The soccer families that we'd been connected to for years were getting a firsthand account of how our lives were changing. At the start, Michelle and I sat at opposite ends of a row, but it got easier over time. Gradually, we moved to sitting next to each other and conversing in a pleasant way. I don't know if I can pinpoint the exact moment that influenced the shift, but here's what comes to mind to explain it as best I can:

1. Therapy has helped me acknowledge my feelings and is teaching me to handle them in a healthy way.

2. It was, and continues to be, important for our children to see a positive example of healing through adversity and maintaining good relationships, even as the healing journey continues.

3. I did my best to stop using the word "awkward" to describe events at which I knew we'd be together. Instead, I started saying things similar to, "It's going to be okay," or, "One more step toward healing." I knew the more I used the word "awkward," the more awkward it would feel to be around

each other, so I wanted to find a strategy to create a different emotion.

4. I've come to terms with the fact that I am divorced. My ex-husband is in a new relationship. My children are loved. I still have the love of my extended family.

5. Choosing peace is important to me. Investing in my mental, emotional, and physical well-being helps to manage my energy and angst that can arise in stressful moments.

People and situations are different. Everyone's healing journey is a personal path and has its own timetable. Relationships may be ripped apart, and your emotions may be too raw for you to think of being in the same room with your ex, in-laws, mutual friends, or a new companion. I get it. The reality is that we were not singing "Kumbaya" at first. We had a lot of feelings to sort through. In fact, if you had told me a year before I started writing this book that I'd be experiencing this part of my divorce story in a more positive way, I'd have said you were crazy.

The most important thing is to put yourself in the best possible position to take care of yourself as you move on, and to show your children that they are still surrounded by love, even if Mom and Dad are not together. Give them the time and space they need to process how they feel. We didn't force the kids to accept their dad's new relationship. James was really good about allowing them to take their time getting adjusted to his having someone new, while nurturing his relationship with each of them the way they needed. It was tough for all of us, and there were times when we were at a stalemate about how to move forward. Our separation was also during COVID lockdown, which may have been a blessing in disguise because it gave us the physical distance we needed. Time and space can help bridge the gap between transitioning from divorce to either parent dating or remarrying. Even though we were physically apart, communication continued as we were sorting out our feelings during a difficult time. The ultimate goal for us, and I'm sure you too, was to get to a good place and to ensure our children were okay.

Sometimes getting to that good place comes in ways you least expect, such as when I was extended an invitation to James and Michelle's wedding. I had accepted the fact that James was in a new relationship. But when the relationship moved from dating to engagement, it was as if the clock were started over again on the emotional processing. It's reasonable to think that each person will move on after divorce, but when it happens, reason may go out the window. It was yet another chapter of closure for me, and I accepted it conceptually, especially because there was time between the engagement and the wedding. But it was hard. I'd heard very little about the wedding from the kids, except the date, mainly because they didn't know how I'd feel about hearing all the details.

I'll be honest. At first, I felt left out because I knew the buzz about the wedding was happening all around me. But, really, why should I be included? This wasn't the family cookout I didn't know about. This was James's wedding, and I was his ex-wife. There was no reason for me to know any more than I did, but that didn't stop the swarm of mixed emotions—from flashbacks of my own wedding to holding the divorce papers in my hand, and all the years in between. Some of the same family and friends who had celebrated us would witness the start of James's new life. So, yeah...not easy.

A few weeks before the wedding, James and I met so I could drop my son off for his week with his dad. He brought up the wedding and mentioned that he didn't want me to feel slighted by not being included, but he hadn't been sure how I'd feel about being a part of it. He wanted me to know that I was welcome to come if I felt comfortable.

The conversation caught me off guard, but I appreciated that he'd even brought it up. I told him so. It was considerate and thoughtful. I wasn't quite sure how to respond, so I thanked him and said I would give it some thought. I don't know many people who would get an invitation to their ex-husband's wedding, let alone consider going.

You may be wondering why I didn't just say, "Thanks, but no thanks," right then. The honest answer is I'm not sure. I rode home, asking myself the same question, analyzing it in my head, and wondering if I could handle being at James's wedding. We'd come a long way, but had I come far enough? My head was spinning.

I called my daughter to talk it over with her. She was just as surprised, but listened and understood my uncertainty. In her mature way, my daughter told me to think about it, make sure my decision was for the right reasons, and one I would be okay with in the long run. She made it clear she would support me either way. I appreciated her compassionate ear and continued to drive home in silence.

The next day, I received a message from Michelle; she asked if we could talk. I had a feeling it was about the wedding, so I made myself available. This time, the conversation was a little different than the call we had before my daughter's party. That call was cordial, and though this one was too, it was also a moment of vulnerability for both of us. We acknowledged that it had not been an easy road for any of us. While I was trying to figure out where I fit in a family that I'd been in for thirty years of my life, Michelle was trying to figure out how to fit into a family that had so much history with me. You could put yourself in either of our shoes and realize how uneasy it was. Here we were, in this less than ideal, yet very common way of being connected, trying to figure out the best path forward with dignity, civility, and grace. My children would become Michelle's stepchildren. Her children would become stepsiblings to mine. My son would have more high school activities and events that we'd all support. There would be other extended family events that we'd all attend. This was the hand we had been dealt, and we were trying to play it the right way for James, for our children, and, most of all, for us as women. I've never had an appetite for reality television or buzz on social media where women tear each other down and act a fool over a relationship or anything else. Therefore, I wanted to make the best of our situation, and Michelle did too.

We expressed this during our conversation and viewed this time as an opportunity to do our best to rise above an extremely difficult situation. She acknowledged that I was still part of the family, and I acknowledged her new place in the family. She, too, assured me that I was welcome to attend the wedding...if I was comfortable and if it felt genuine. We ended the conversation on a positive note, and she left it to me to decide. After the conversation, I sat with the thought of the invitation. I wanted to say yes, but I needed to think it over.

Admittedly, I was torn. On one hand, I considered attending because of the conversation Michelle and I had, and with the idea that this would be the perfect chance to demonstrate what rising above adversity looked like. James and Michelle were happy, and my children would get a firsthand glimpse of how to turn a trying situation into something good. After all, our kids were in the wedding and happy for their dad. In a sense, they were leading the way, turning our situation around for the good. If I attended the wedding, I would get to see the family I still loved dearly.

Wait! This wasn't a barbecue or birthday party, as my sister, Toshah, had reminded me. This was my ex-husband's wedding, It was one thing to have a heartfelt conversation over the phone with Michelle, but quite another to sit through vows, the first toast, the spoon tap on the glasses to initiate a kiss, and all the other formalities. I had to play out all the scenarios in my head and truthfully acknowledge how I would feel in those moments.

Yes, I was in therapy and working through my emotions prior to this point. I had friends and family, including my children, who were sources of support for me. I'd made self-care a priority in order to nurture myself to a place of wholeness. But did I really think I could detach myself enough to be just a guest, like everyone else? Between close family weighing in and my own vacillating thoughts about whether to attend or not, I was overwhelmed. These weren't the feelings that a guest should have at a wedding, so I politely declined. The moment I did, I felt a sense of relief, which was a sign that I'd made the right decision. Besides, this was *their* day; they should be allowed to enjoy it to the fullest.

On the day of the wedding, I went to dinner with family. I did my best to keep myself occupied, and it was important for me to be surrounded by a tribe of support. Though I was relieved that I decided not to attend the wedding, I had no idea about the roller-coaster ride I would take leading up to that day. Let's just say I don't like roller coasters, but I'll talk about that later.

Yes, the family ties are certainly different, and we're taking one step at a time to keep growing into and getting comfortable with our new norm. Decide what this looks like for you based on your situation. James and I have a good relationship; we are connected through our children, family conversations, and occasional events. We have a family text thread with our kids, my sister, and my niece; we share jokes, pictures, sports updates, and the latest news. We keep it lighthearted and fun, which is something we can all enjoy and appreciate.

Since every relationship after divorce is different, you may not need or want to have anything to do with your ex or extended family, let alone a new companion. That's okay. Set whatever boundaries you need to remain emotionally healthy and to move forward in the best way that gives you closure, peace, and joy.

" Enjoy the now, and let now determine if you'll go to next. "

Chapter
4

The Dating Game

I have mixed feelings about dating after divorce. I know that as long as I'm breathing, there is hope for the right person to come along. But at the present moment, I'm not in a long-term relationship. I'm completely okay with this because having my own space has been good for me. Being by myself has given me the chance to reflect and figure out what I do and don't like, how I want to spend my time, and what peace feels like. It's important for women, in particular, to invest this time in themselves; it is time well spent, whether you are divorced or not.

Shortly after the divorce, there was a part of me that dreaded the thought of being out there in the dating scene. Actually, I don't even know if that's what I should call it because that sounds so committed. I hear the buzz about the small pool of good men (my preference) who are available and have had conversations with my married friends who say they'd hate to be in my shoes—out in the dating world—these days. That's enough to make me approach being single with some trepidation, but I'm also experiencing a level of freedom that some of them desire. It's not that they're in unhealthy or unfulfilling relationships. It just means they have someone else to consider when thinking about self-discovery, goals, and dreams. I'm not yet ready for a serious relationship, but I'm open to meeting new people, developing friendships, and enjoying good companionship.

I've been out of the dating scene for over thirty years. Wow, has it changed! I remember the days when a close friend or family member would introduce you to a friend, you'd double-date a few times, solo date for a while, and if there was a connection, you'd call yourselves a couple. Or you'd go out with friends, meet someone at a club or restaurant, exchange numbers, and go from there.

In 2019, I was having a conversation with my sister, Toshah, and two of my cousins; they are all single and were part of my support system as I transitioned into single life. This was shortly after my separation agreement was finalized. We were talking about going out together to have fun and meet people. We were excited and talked about getting in shape and getting our wardrobes together so we'd be ready to hit the social scene. We had it all planned. Then COVID hit; we were in quarantine, so there was no going out. Our plans were squashed, as was my interest in meeting anyone. Besides, given the critical nature of the pandemic, meeting people was the last thing on my mind.

After we realized meeting people in person was not going to happen for a while (we had no clue just how long "a while" would turn out to be), my sister suggested trying a couple of dating apps. She mentioned a few to consider, and I'm glad she did because I had no clue where to start. I gave it some thought, but not much effort. I must admit that I was resistant to it because in some ways it felt weird. Creating a profile, adding your pictures, and then having random strangers checking you out felt a bit strange and somewhat impersonal. *Is it worth my time? How much do I share? Is it safe?* These were the questions that came up because I was in unfamiliar territory. One might argue that it's the same thing as meeting someone new in person. I suppose that's true, but digital was a whole new world for me.

I eventually signed up for the free accounts on three apps, checked in sporadically, and had a few cordial conversations here and there, but that's about it. I'd converse with someone one day, and then they'd be gone from my profile the next, meaning they unmatched with me. How dare they! Or I'd converse with someone for about a week or so, and then it would just go cold. I was curious whether those people were just as resistant as I was about giving time and energy to the apps, or if my profile just wasn't that interesting. *Was it something I said or didn't say during the conversation that was a turnoff?* Then there was all the inner dialogue I was having with myself when I got unmatched or didn't hit it off with someone. Even though I wasn't ready for a serious relationship, I still bombarded my brain with thoughts similar to, *Will I ever find companionship? Is there something wrong with me? This is a joke.*

Whatever the case, those experiences were enough for me to develop a lackadaisical attitude about investing my time in the apps. I now know those thoughts were extreme and irrational. But in the moments when I was trying something totally new, and quite uneasy about, the irrational sounded rational.

Then my sister reminded me to pump the brakes and just go with the flow. I was overthinking every-thing about using the dating apps, trying to analyze too much, and at times, second-guessing myself. I was determined to confidently move into single life, so I wasn't about to let a dating app get in the way of my goal! I had to shift the focus from doubting myself, to being confident that who I was and how I pre-sented myself in my profile was more than enough. If someone unmatched me, it meant I wasn't for them, and they weren't for me.

Not to mention the fact that at the time, we were still in the middle of a global pandemic, so the likelihood of connecting with someone and meeting for coffee, drinks, or dinner was low. The apps were still on my phone, but during COVID, I spent less time on them and more time on me.

If you're trying to figure out if dating apps are for you, I would say be open to them when you're ready. It's similar to having multiple ways to get to a single destination. You may be used to traveling the same route to get to where you're trying to go, but a detour may force you to go a different way. It might feel strange because you're not used to going a new way, but if you relax and follow your GPS, you'll get to the destination at the right time.

Ironically, I'm the same person who fusses back at the GPS when I think it's giving me directions that don't make sense. Sometimes I feel the same frustration when I'm swiping through the app. This is a reminder—for me, as well—to exercise patience on many levels! I realize, in today's world, there are multiple ways to meet people. Dating apps happen to be one of them, but managing three apps was a lot for me. For my own sanity and to manage my time better, I deleted two of the apps, kept one, and upgraded it to a paid membership.

If you choose to use a dating app, I suggest, before just jumping in, that you spend some time reflecting to become clear on your *whys*. What are you hoping to accomplish by using the dating app? What are your dating goals in general? My goal is to find people with shared interests, have good conversations, enjoy dinners, coffee, or shows, and have fun while doing those things. I'm not actively seeking a steady boyfriend or husband at the moment. Instead, I'm looking to establish friendships.

Take your time, see if there's a good vibe between you and those you meet through the app. If you happen to narrow it down to a single person of interest, the next level of the relationship will show up at the right time if it's meant to be. Your goals may be similar to mine or totally different, and that's okay as long as you've defined yours. Remember, there are lots of dating apps out there. Some are just for a quick hookup, others are faith-based, and still others are interest-focused, like apps for gamers, for outdoorsy types, or for people within a certain age range. Because there are so many options, it's important to figure out your *whys* and then choose the app that's right for you.

While I'm focusing here on the nuances of using dating apps, I feel it important to mention that everything I share about dating apps is equally applicable to other forms of dating or meeting people after divorce.

The interpersonal nuances are the same, no matter the type of relationship you are seeking.

If you choose dating apps, however, you may also need a lesson in the lingo used on them. I quickly found that out! Shortly after I signed on to the three apps my sister recommended, I was scrolling through one of them, and a gentleman attracted my attention, so I read his profile. As I read, I was drawn by the fact that he said he was "Poly." I thought, *Cool! Something we have in common!* My high school was Baltimore Polytechnic Institute, which we affectionately call "Poly." I started a conversation by asking him what year he graduated. After a few messages back and forth, he realized I had no idea what poly (polyamorous) meant, so he politely informed me that he was open to multiple romantic relationships at the same time. All I could do was respond with, "Ohhhhh," and a laughing emoji; then I laughed at myself for being so green. Needless to say, I didn't continue the conversation, but it may have been perfectly okay for someone else to engage further.

I later did a search while writing this book and found a dictionary full of dating terms and slang on askmen.com. Who knew? It may be worth checking out if you're interested in pursuing dating apps for companionship.

As women, we may also be holding on to outdated norms about who approaches whom when there is interest. My friend Jerome and I had an enlightening discussion about how dating apps have changed the game in terms of who makes the first move. Before dating apps, Jerome said that if he was in a room full of people, most women did not approach him; instead, they expected him to initiate contact. He went on to say that he thought this stemmed from what our mothers, grandmothers, and aunts taught us. In their eras, it was unheard of for a woman to approach a man first; back then, the roles men and women played in relationships were strictly defined.

Well, things have certainly changed. Women are bolder and more empowered to start conversations not only through dating apps, but also in person. I've initiated contact through the apps and had no problem with it. But I've been in very few situations to test this same boldness in public, except the time I went out to celebrate my sister's birthday. I was sitting at the bar with my sister and cousin on one side of me, and a guy and his friends on the other. I started having a conversation with the guy closest to me. Eventually, both our parties were talking and laughing, and the guy and I ended up talking the whole time.

As we were preparing to leave, I was going to graciously get up, exchange pleasant goodbyes, and head out the door with my family. Well, my sister thought I should exchange more than pleasantries! She wrote my name and number on a napkin, slid it to the guy I was talking to, and said something similar to, "Here you go. That way, y'all can continue your conversation later!" He gladly accepted the napkin and gave me his information too. He and I laughed and loosely mentioned meeting again to have a drink. As my sister, cousin, and I left the bar, we chuckled about my sister's smooth move.

I hadn't planned to exchange numbers. Not because I was being timid, but because I wasn't really interested in conversation with him beyond the bar talk. I made note of my sister's napkin play, though. I might need to use that in the future!

Just understand, regardless of how you go about meeting people, if you wait for people of interest to reach out to you first, you may miss out. While I'm content with initiating contact and showing interest, I also want a man to show me that he's interested. I want to feel as if I'm being pursued, even in this liberated age. If I'm the one doing all the initiating, I will likely interpret this as the other person being a narcissist or not interested. That may be unfair, but if there is limited communication, then I'm left with my own assumptions.

Dating and apps aside, I've taken full advantage of being in my own space. In addition to growing and learning about myself, being single has given me time to think about what's important when it comes to relationship building, such as focusing on friendship first. At the very least, you may be gaining a new friend with no heavy emotional or physical commitment issues. At most, you'll be starting from a solid foundation if the friendship turns into something more.

Getting to know someone requires availability, not just being free from your marriage, but free emotionally and timewise. Divorce is a loss, and there are various stages you will go through before coming to terms and accepting it as your new normal. If you're angry with your ex, depressed, or grieving over the change in your family dynamic, you are not emotionally available to someone else.

This is where therapy can help. I am an advocate of therapy and have regular sessions. At first, therapy helped me get through my feelings about losing my marriage. Now, it helps me embrace areas of growth, and it is a regular part of my wellness routine.

A person can have all the time in the world, but still be emotionally connected to someone else, or not healed enough from a previous relationship to move on to another. Maybe there is no other emotional connection, but the person works all the time, which leaves little to no opportunity to spend time together. You may meet someone who has very little physical energy for conversation or spending time together. Perhaps you, or the person you're interested in, share custody and are responsible for getting the kids to sports and other events, or you just want to devote quality time to your children. Being present for our children is important, so availability to others may be less of a priority, at least initially. These scenarios are considerations for both parties when establishing a new relationship.

I was having a conversation with a friend who made it known that he was "single and available." I acknowledged the same because I had no emotional connection with my ex, and I had time freedom. We exchanged several text conversations for a while and finally agreed to meet for dinner. We had a great time and good conversation. In the days and weeks following dinner, we texted, and he asked several times when we were going to get together again. Each time, I replied that I was open and attempted to narrow down a day and time, but there was no follow-up or effort on his part to make it happen. After seeing this pattern of behavior, I took it as a sign that he really wasn't available, for whatever reason; pressing it further was a waste of my time.

When I asked my friend Jerome for his insight into this behavior, he confirmed what I already knew. He said, "It means he's not one hundred percent vested in you. If I'm interested in a woman, she's going to know it."

This is why self-reflection time is key. It helps us to get clear on not only what we want in a relationship—love or just companionship—but also our worth. Knowing our worth helps us avoid the pitfalls from being so desperate for companionship that we ignore signs of disinterest and pursue someone at all costs. It doesn't matter what you're told about someone's availability. As my dear friend Trish often says, a person can show you better than he can tell you. If their actions don't match what they say, then they're probably not as available as they claim to be. You have to decide how vested *you* will be.

Availability is reciprocal. It's best for both parties to be free of emotional ties and willing to invest the time if building a relationship, on any level, is important. Spending time with myself taught me that I was not willing to put more energy into a man than he was willing to invest in me.

One other aspect of relationship building that became important to me was conversations beyond text messages because, in my opinion, communicating solely through texts provides only a limited view of the person with whom you are texting. In fact, I didn't realize how much of a pet peeve this was for me because texting is such a part of our communications culture. I text with my friends and family all the time, but there is something different about having an actual conversation with someone you're getting to know.

I recall several instances in which I asked a guy, after going back and forth for days through texts, to either give me a call or tell me a good time for me to call him. That question meant it was time to pause the texting and talk over the phone, right? No. Instead, I'd receive another text or emoji. That drove me nuts! I don't know if that response was motivated by avoidance, fear of communicating, unavailability, or a combination of all three, but it was annoying as hell. After a few reminders that I was open to phone calls, with no acknowledgment of that fact by text or an actual phone call, I stopped communicating with him. He never responded to that at all.

For all I know, what may have been important to him was *not* having phone calls and *only* communicating through texts. But when there's no substantive conversation, it's hard to know what matters to the other person and how you can meet in the middle, or identify deal breakers altogether.

All this made me realize that availability and verbal communication are very basic things that are important to me. However, you might be okay with only texting or occasional calls. You may define availability differently or determine other things are more important to you. Everyone has their own expectations; this should not be confused with desires.

One day, my cousin Brian and I were sitting in my kitchen and talking about dating. He shared that desire is something we want deeply, but may not receive. He explained that you may desire to spend time with friends once a month to catch up and recharge. Yet you may be reluctant to share this with your significant other because either you don't think you deserve the time, or your companion will feel slighted. Therefore, you don't receive what you desire.

However, expectation is what we anticipate receiving or how we anticipate engaging in various aspects of a relationship. A clear statement of expectation to your companion might sound similar to: "You can *expect* that I'll take time for myself once a month to be with my friends, and I *expect* you to be okay with that. Is this something we can agree on?" It's a clear statement that sets the tone for how time is spent within the relationship. You should encourage your companion to share his expectations as well. Stating expectations can spark dialogues that establish norms with which each person can live, or it may force a decision point if they can't.

Brian said he'd rather have a woman be clear about expectations, and he'd honor her by doing the same, even for the smallest things. That way, neither person has to assume anything and risk disappointing the other. At the very least, both parties can have discussions about whether the expectations are realistic and work together to create what works best for them. Discussing expectations is healthy, no matter what stage of relationship building you're in. It can be as simple as deciding how dates will be arranged at the beginning of a new relationship or discussing how disagreements will be handled in more committed relationships.

For me, physically talking to a person is a form of communication that I expect, and it is a rich part of connecting with another human being. My sister and I joke all the time about communication because she's content with text messages. In fact, if you text her too much she just might ignore you for a minute, until she's ready to engage. Oh, do we have some good laughs about this! But, seriously, she's very good with being in the moment and having fun, and she reminds me to do the same. She's single, and I appreciate the perspective she gives me on how to embrace this moment of my life happily and freely.

Decide what matters to you, and keep that at the forefront of your mind when getting to know someone; continue to do so as the relationship evolves.

Exploring what you're looking for in a companion, and the type of companionship you want, is crucial. Giving it some thought before you start dating after divorce will serve you well; it just may help you avoid settling for someone who doesn't align with what you want. Jerome also reminded me of a very candid difference between men and women: some men want sex, and some women expect men to buy them things, so relationships are transactional.

The reality is that some women just want sex too, and they may not need a man to buy them anything.

It goes back to knowing your *whys* and being up-front about it with the people you meet; expect the same in return. On the dating app, I met a guy who told me he'd never been married and knew he wanted that for himself. He asked if I saw myself getting married again, and my response was that I honestly didn't know. It certainly wasn't at the top of my mind, especially after a nearly thirty-year marriage. I didn't want to mislead him; if his sole purpose for dating was to find a wife...well, I wasn't the one. We respected each other's position and stayed in touch for a while, but eventually we stopped communicating. It was for the best.

I had dinner with a dear friend, Denise, before my separation was final, and I shared that I was not looking forward to starting over. The thought of getting to know someone new, their getting to know me, and finding out all our idiosyncrasies was something to which I wasn't looking forward. She suggested that I write a list of things that I'd be looking for in a mate, so I did.

I thought about the areas of my life that are important to me and how I spend my time—has same faith values, family man, loves and honors me and my children, can engage in stimulating conversation, is health conscious and physically fit, is handsome and well-groomed, likes to have fun and enjoys travel, and is financially stable (legitimately). It's also important to me to connect with someone who believes in and supports my goals, some of which are beyond what is visible to the natural eye. Yes, it can be scary to dream big, but it's not my ideal situation if I have to constantly work to get someone else to buy into those dreams. That can be exhausting. I'm fully aware that anyone I meet may have a list of his own, and I welcome exploring the compatibility. By the way, I also added that he'd be able to cook, but that's negotiable!

If you haven't written a list for yourself, take some time to do it. It will help you to create the standard for yourself as you start meeting people. Think about what's important to you. Here are some areas to consider. Feel free to use these or create your own list.

1. Faith/religion.

2. Education.

3. Travel/leisure.

4. Family relationships/values.

5. Financial health.

6. Wellness/self-care approach.

7. Hobbies.

8. Physical attraction.

9. Displays of affection.

10. Profession.

Be as specific as you can, but be willing to distinguish nice-to-haves from the must-haves. Most of all, be true to yourself and have fun with it. Now, don't pull your list out on the first few dates! The more time you spend getting to know someone—listening, observing, and having organic conversations that help you figure out where the person stands on the things that are important to you—the healthier your relationship will be if you choose to pursue one. Once your must-haves are defined, don't settle for someone who doesn't align with them. If you want a partner who enjoys travel, but you meet someone who has no interest in leaving the state, it may not be the best fit.

This may sound old-fashioned, but I'm also attracted to someone who still believes in chivalry; though, my friend Jerome believes that it's "one of the biggest lies outside of Santa Claus!" He happens to think that chivalry is based on what women were taught to expect from a man back in the old days, but that it is no longer as relevant, now that times have changed. I happen to disagree. I like when a man holds the door for me, helps me with my coat, and walks on the outer part of the curb when we're together. Don't get me wrong; I can do these things for myself. However, there's something endearing about this display of attentiveness. After having general conversations with other men, I've discovered many men, as well, still believe in chivalry.

After you've made a list of what you're looking for in a companion, be realistic and identify where you're willing to be flexible. The likelihood that someone will meet everything on your list is slim, so you must decide what the deal breakers are and on what you're willing to compromise. You may even decide to have one list for friendships or casual relationships, and another for a long-term, more committed relationship.

In one of our sessions, my therapist asked me to think about what type of relationship I was looking for, at least initially—a committed relationship, a purely physical one, or a casual hangout. I appreciated her asking the question because it was all part of defining what was important and how I would approach the dating scene. I knew that I was not looking for anything serious right away, and I wasn't comfortable with a purely physical relationship at the start, even though that is an enticing option. That left me with the casual hangout, and I am okay with that for now. But I also realize that my desires may change, and I'll adjust to that when the time comes.

While a physical relationship has not been a priority, I can't deny my lack of physical intimacy. If I'm honest, physical intimacy makes me a little nervous because I liken my absent sex life to a common phrase in many organizations about paid leave: Use it or lose it! Will I remember what to do? Okay, I know that's silly. It's like riding a bike! Although, the last time I rode a bike was a few years ago, and that was the first time I'd been on one in years. I was wobbly, and it felt awkward for a bit, but the basics came back to me. I was tired during and after the ride, so I guess it's a fitting analogy to sex!

Seriously, I'm older, and my body has changed, so I may require a little more effort and attention to have a pleasurable experience when the time comes. And, listen, the hormonal changes that cause night sweats (and day sweats too) aren't sexy. I can manage my sweat outbreaks on my own, even though they drive me crazy at times. But I can't help but wonder if these changes will show up during a romantic moment, and whether I'll be so focused on managing the sweats that I won't enjoy the sex.

I have to be vulnerable enough to communicate all this to a partner and to be open about what would make me feel comfortable. While this type of conversation is about establishing companionship and enjoying a physical relationship as a single woman, many married women have these same concerns. The most ideal situation is to be with someone who understands you, your needs, and is thoughtful about creating an experience you both enjoy. After all, your companion may have concerns of his own, and you need to be sensitive to those.

I was having an enlightening conversation with a dear friend who expressed a new level of sexual freedom after divorce. Not in a promiscuous way, but rather a new understanding of her body, her needs, and how to enjoy sex in ways she had not before. It was a juicy conversation, to say the least, and I was on the edge of my seat as an attentive listener. It was as if I were listening to a steamy audiobook! I appreciated her openness about things women don't often talk about when it comes to our femininity, intimacy, and sexuality. All can be points of liberation for many women after divorce.

It can be intimidating to talk about these things, especially if you've never had those conversations before with a mate, your friend circle, or even your children. We may be embarrassed, naïve, or holding on to the belief that we shouldn't have these conversations. I've been a little of all three at times. I believe every woman should be able to connect with her physical needs, either through information from her doctor, sacred talks with friends, or an openness to self-pleasure. Then you can communicate those needs to a partner if the relationship expands to physical intimacy. I'm discovering a lot in this area. Let's just say, a girl's gotta do what a girl's gotta do.

I remember the day my coach and mentor, Lisa Nichols, got married. I watched clips that were shared on social media, and the wedding was stunning. There were vibrant touches of red throughout the venue, flowers, and decorations. Lisa wore the most gorgeous red dress; her hair was braided, twisted into an updo, and adorned with a beaded headdress.

No, not a traditional white gown and veil, as we're so accustomed to seeing. She had the guests wear white instead. I marveled at how beautiful she was. This was so Lisa! She's always been an unapologetic game changer, which is what drew me to her in the first place.

Leading up to the wedding, I caught glimpses of her life with her then fiancé. She marveled at him, as he did with her. You could see the love, affection, and pure joy they experienced with one another. What I love about the story of their love is that she often talked about being in her fifties and having challenges in relationships, yet she prepared herself first so that she would be ready for the man of her dreams. As a speaker, author, and coach, she taught me and so many others how to work on ourselves so we could show up and play big in the world. Moving beyond fear, not dimming your light, changing your mindset, defining what you want, and believing those things could come to pass were all parts of the lessons she taught. Relationships were part of the lessons too. It was no surprise to see the glow of her love in everything she did. First, love for herself, and then the love for her man.

Earlier that same day, before I started looking at all the clips and pictures of the wedding, I was a little frustrated. This was during the time when I'd reengaged with the membership version of the dating apps, which gave me the ability to see more profiles, not just blurred images. I was back to striking up casual conversations that seemed interesting with some of the matches. We'd message back and forth, and then the conversation would go cold. I started wondering again if this was a waste of time, and if it was, what other ways I could meet people. Then there was one conversation that was really engaging and lasted more than a week, which may not sound like a lot of time, but that's like an eternity in the app world. We exchanged numbers, continued to have great conversations over the phone, went out a few times, and enjoyed each other's company. We had a good vibe.

He was available, had no problem with verbal communication, and said that he appreciated the same from me. As exciting as it was to connect with someone, it was a little scary too. It had been so long since I'd received that kind of attention from a man; in some ways, it felt strange. And, yes, I was nervous about the first date! As I was driving to the restaurant where we agreed to meet, I was giving myself pep talks—"This is a first date," "Be yourself," "You look gorgeous," and "It'll be okay"—that helped calm the butterflies in my stomach.

As it turned out, we had a great time, and a second date the next day. We continued to talk through texts and on the phone for a few days after we went out. Then silence. Suddenly, there was no communication from him and no response to my texts or the few calls

I made to check on him. I decided that I was not going to reach out anymore.

Then I received a long text message with all the sweet words about me and my beauty—*rolling eyes*—but his availability was limited. I'll admit that getting a detailed text felt like a cop-out, especially after many phones call, but it told me all I needed to know. My response was short and cordial.

Did I enjoy the attention for the brief time we connected? Yes. Was I craving it so much that I was willing to invest more time in him than he in me? No. My motto was "Keep it moving."

This is the reason I suggest you identify your *whys* for dating. You can use them as a measure to guide your response to people as different situations arise. If you know your goal is to casually start meeting people, then you will easily blow off the connections that don't go far. My *whys* have come in handy on a number of occasions when I found myself over-thinking or asking myself whether I could be in a relationship with a person just by looking at pro-file pictures, personal descriptions, or going on a few dates. *Remember, Ericka, you're just trying to meet new people, go out, and have fun. Don't claim a serious relation-ship before you're ready. Ahhh, right. Note to self: If you decide to move on, your list will remind you of what you're moving toward.*

Of course, if you're looking for a serious relationship or a new spouse right away, then you may be focused on your list with more intensity. Be sure, however, to place as much emphasis on doing the personal work on yourself so that you'll be ready for what you're asking for when you find it.

I'll continue with the dating apps. I'm not sure where things will go, but here's what I do know—I don't have to figure it out at this stage, and I don't want to. I've created a new mantra as I continue this dating journey: "Enjoy the now, and let now determine if you'll go to next." "Next" can be as simple as the next text message, the next phone call, the next date, or the next level to a physical or committed relationship. It can also be an opportunity to end all efforts at building a relationship, or at the very least a reduction in communication on any level. If the connection doesn't feel right between you and another person, be an advocate for your time and energy. Recognize that "next" might be taking the exit ramp.

I went out with a guy who was nice, and we had decent conversations on the phone. We met once for drinks and had a really good time, but it never worked out when we planned a second date. He'd say, "Oh, we have to get together again soon," and I'd respond, "Yeah, we do," but we never really committed to anything concrete. Though he was nice, there was something I wasn't feeling, and he may have been thinking the same. It got to the point that

I no longer made an effort to call or text him, and he wasn't reaching out to me either. It was a mutual end, and I was perfectly okay with that.

I started the personal-growth journey of thinking about what I wanted for my life before James and I were legally separated. By the time our divorce was final, I was already beginning to enjoy time freedom. Going to lunch or dinner alone, hanging with family and friends, getting massages, or binge-watching Netflix with popcorn and wine were simple things I enjoyed. I was getting used to doing them on my own. I loved buying myself fresh flowers, but when I got a bouquet from someone other than my kids or me, I had to work at being open to it. It had been so long since I'd received a gift from a man that I'd forgotten what that feeling of excitement was like. They were beautiful, and I appreciated the thoughtful gesture. Besides, it was nice to feel giddy and smile.

If someone wants to give you flowers, buy you dinner, or treat you to a movie, let them; allow yourself to enjoy it. Try not to be suspicious or question their intent, unless there's something in the relationship that leads you to believe the gift brings with it the expectation of getting something in return. Then you'd have to make some serious decisions about that relationship.

You may have several thoughts, concerns, and questions about dating after divorce. There's nothing wrong with that. In fact, it's good if you do because it encourages you to create the standards that will help you when you do meet someone. The choice is yours. Whether you decide to keep it casual or committed is up to you. Not only should you be clear on your dating *whys*, but those that you meet should be too.

As I meet men, I'm up-front about friendship, fun, and allowing things to happen organically; I ask what their expectations are as well. This way, there is no confusion about what both parties expect from the relationship. If those expectations don't align, you can break it off before getting too far into a relationship that won't serve either of you well. Whatever you do, don't settle for someone whom you don't enjoy or who doesn't treat you the way you want and deserve.

I will admit there are times when I ask myself if I will find love again. I believe when the time is right, I will. I'm in my early fifties, so I know that I have more years behind me than in front of me. But I'm on the journey to explore and intentional about enjoying it as I go. I remind myself to be in the moment and allow everything else to take care of itself.

It's okay if you're looking for Mr. Right...or Mr. Right Now.

❝❝ If there *is*
something
you've been
longing to do,
give yourself
permission
to do it. ❞❞

Chapter 5

Use It for Good

When I graduated from college, I wasn't sure what I was going to do with my psychology degree. To be honest, I declared psychology as a major on a whim because it sounded interesting. However, the more classes I took in the major, the more I enjoyed it, so I thought I'd become a psychologist. But after graduating, the immediate goal was to find a decent job as soon as possible. I went to work in the health-care industry, where I stayed for close to twenty unplanned years! It was in those later years of my corporate career that I realized I wasn't fulfilled, and something was missing. As I shared in my first book, *Pathway to Purpose: Find It. Follow It. Fulfill It.*, that empty feeling led me on a journey to self-discovery.

What I realized during that time was that I was a magnet for other women to share their highs and lows. I was sought for counsel as my colleagues and friends were experiencing life on different levels, and being an ear for them or presenting new insight on what they were going through was a space that felt exciting and natural. More importantly, it seemed to be impactful for them and rewarding for me to know I was making a difference. I realized my passion was to help women move beyond doubts, fears, insecurities, and past failures to be the best version of themselves and to pursue their own dreams. This is what motivated me to start my coaching business, TruSynergy, LLC.

I have to say, when I took the leap to start the business, I had a completely different name for it, but a trademark snafu forced me to go back to the drawing board to come up with a new name. I remember the day as if it were yesterday. I received a phone call from a trademark attorney who politely notified me that the name on my promotional materials, website, and filings was off-limits. I was distraught and beat myself up for not being as thorough as I thought. I had no idea what to do.

At approximately forty-five days before the launch of my new company, that was a temporary moment of defeat for me. I had come so far. I had to literally stop in my tracks, rethink, and reset. I allowed myself the much-needed time to cry and be frustrated; then I sat down to think of a new name. In hindsight, this experience was much like my divorce. Feeling as if I were on the right path for my life, only to realize that I wasn't, which forced me to recreate what had become familiar.

The beauty of that snafu was that it allowed me to think more carefully about what I wanted my clients to experience after engaging with me. My mission had always been focused on guiding women to experience mind, body, and spirit wellness in every area of their lives. This is the kind of synergy that I believed would help women discover their true essence and allow them to live a more fulfilled life. The more I sifted through this in my mind, the more right the name TruSynergy felt. In fact, it was a better fit and had more meaning than the original name, which shall not be spoken!

I turned my lack of fulfillment in my professional career into a successful coaching business because I had my own difficult life experiences to navigate through, and I used those experiences to create a new life for myself. As I started to focus more on my business, I learned that dealing with my own challenges would become an integral part of my connection with my clients and the strategies I developed to serve them.

Up until the divorce, I often referred to my bullying during childhood, an inappropriate incident with an adult male whom I trusted, an emotionally abusive relationship in college, and the challenges in my corporate career. I wanted to share my own struggles with confidence and low self-esteem. In fact, I created the P.A.S.T. strategy to process those experiences. I use it often for myself and my clients.

1. Pain Points (P)—Put all those pain points under a microscope.

2. Assess (A)—Evaluate how your behavior dictates your life as a result of the pain points.

3. Stronghold (S)—Connect the stronghold, or emotional component, of the pain points.

4. Transformation (T)—Shift to a transformational moment in which the pain points are used as an opportunity for personal growth and helping others.

As emotionally challenging as it has been, the divorce gave me an area of focus to share with new clients. Divorce is a new pain point, and the P.A.S.T. formula is a valuable tool to help process the behaviors and emotions associated with it. Is it easy? No, but it's certainly enlightening and rewarding because it helps you to connect with the challenging areas of your life. More importantly, it shifts you into creating something better from the challenges. Divorce is certainly not something that I thought would be part of my life story. However, the experience has given me a brand-new perspective on how to live beyond a failed marriage and how to discover a level of independence that's exciting. Our life experiences don't belong just to us, but to the people who will benefit from the testimonies behind our stories.

Divorce is a time of family crisis, and I hated that we were experiencing it. Sometimes we need to shift our energy toward something that feels better than the space we're in. My business was that shift for me, and it served as an outlet. Instead of taking a step back from it, I leaned into it more, both for me and my clients. I was using the same strategies for myself that I was sharing with clients, and that collective experience made the coaching partnership that much richer because I could relate. My business also gave me the opportunity to focus on something other than what was going on in my family, so I viewed it as a way to escape. I wasn't in denial about what was going on with my family, but in the moments when I was working with my clients, I didn't have to think about my problems. I strongly believe that every speaking engagement, client, conference, and hour spent writing were therapeutic outlets.

I also enjoy the fact that I can freely manage the time for my business without having to check in or clear my schedule with a significant other. Sure, I have to coordinate with my ex-husband to make sure my son is covered when I travel or have an event, especially if it's during a week when he's scheduled to be with me. I'm grateful that our co-parenting relationship allows each of us the flexibility when we need it. But other than that, I don't have to explain myself or get anyone else to understand and buy into what I'm doing. That's a damn good feeling.

One day, I was in the nail salon when I overheard a woman talking to her technician about her divorce. We were the only customers in the salon at the time, so it was very easy to hear her conversation. Her divorce was recent, and she talked about having to get used to her ex-husband not being around, even though he was still assisting her with fixing things around the house. I could hear the sadness and uncertainty in her voice, a tone I recognized all too well.

As I got up from my station to go wash my hands, I politely said, "Excuse me, I don't mean to eavesdrop, but I'm recently divorced too, and acceptance of the divorce gets easier." I wasn't sure how she'd respond. Perhaps she'd tell me to mind my business, even though she wasn't secretive about her conversation. Or maybe she'd find it helpful to hear. I was relieved when she thanked me for sharing and said she really appreciated the comment. She also mentioned that this was her second divorce. I couldn't help but wonder what other emotions come along with going through divorce more than once. Regardless, I wanted her to know that she wasn't alone.

This brief conversation was a reminder that my divorce was not just my story, but one that I would share with other women who, perhaps, have the same trepidation about life after divorce as I had. As I discussed in chapter one, I was afraid of divorce for so many reasons, but I'm a living witness that it's possible to find joy and peace on the other side of it. I've added this part of my life to my coach's toolbox, which allows me to serve a new population of women who are already divorced or in the process of getting one.

Engaging in a coaching relationship can breathe new life into a woman who's looking for direction on how to start over and how to do it with grace. Moving on with grace doesn't mean there won't be times when you don't feel your best, or situations that will trigger your emotions. It means, when those moments come, you will give yourself permission to be in that space, and you vow to keep working to release the things that are keeping you from being whole. A coaching partnership can support this. As a coach, being relatable to your clients creates an authentic experience that's built on trust. That trust helps provide a foundation for the client's transformation. I get to share the challenges and the pain of my divorce, but also strategies for resilience that remind other women that they can get through it.

Going through a divorce can sometimes make you feel powerless because you're no longer in control of the thing you thought would last forever. It's one thing to navigate a new family dynamic with your spouse, kids, and your extended family, but carving out your own identity may require work, especially if your focus was always on your spouse and children, leaving little time or energy for investing in yourself.

Of all the women I've coached, only two were divorced. In both cases, a good portion of the work we did together was related to building confidence and establishing their identities outside of the marriage.

After my divorce, I had to give myself the time and space to get to know me again because I'd never lived on my own. I needed to figure out who I was apart from the family to which I'd been accustomed. I learned how to nurture myself; that was, and continues to be, liberating. Self-care is an important part of the healing process, and I'll talk more about that later. Some women don't know how to figure out what their happiness looks like, mainly because their mental, emotional, or physical space is so cluttered that they can't see how to move to the next level. This is why a coach can be a beneficial part of the healing process after divorce.

I remember when I started following author and motivational speaker Lisa Nichols on social media. It was quite an experience to be in the virtual space with so many other like-minded people who were ready for something new and exciting in their lives. By the comments in various posts and during the virtual events she held, it was clear that we all had baggage and burdens to release in order to embrace something new. Lisa created such a safe virtual space that I decided to invest in her other coaching services in person, attending a conference in Atlanta, enrolling in her business academy, and volunteering at her Abundance Now book release in New York. She was smart, authentic, compassionate, and energetic. Most of all, she told relatable stories about her life and practical solutions that helped her move from a life of scarcity to an abundance mindset. This allowed her to become the powerhouse coach, author, and speaker she is today.

This is what resonated with me. Lisa could tell her audience and clients about how to have a better life because she had many experiences when life was a struggle. She figured out how to overcome those struggles, and the strategies she used became a part of a dynamic coaching platform from which I actively learned. Not only was I learning how to expand my view of possibilities for myself, but I was also understanding how to be a relatable coach with integrity and compassion. Studying under Lisa helped me to see how important it is to connect with my clients in an authentic way. I must share where I've been and how my journey relates to theirs. It's easier to help other women see that it's possible to bounce back from divorce because I've gone through it.

Working with Lisa, with other coaches, and establishing relationships with many different people gave me a sense of connection. This was an essential part of my continued healing, so I encourage you to find supportive communities and align with people and things that will lift you up. One of the worst things you can do when you're trying to get over the loss of your marriage is to hang around people who are always negative. Instead of encouraging you and lifting you up, their energy drains you. Choose your circle wisely. And, of course, coaching provides a safe space that gives you the freedom to identify the barriers holding you back from your joy, and the tools to map out a path forward.

My ex-husband supported my business venture early on, but as we got closer to separation, and before the divorce, our main focus was on the kids. I discussed very little about my business, and he didn't seem interested enough to ask. I don't think either one of us was in the emotional space to care about sharing. In order to have something to be excited about and look forward to, I decided to stay in my silo about the business and use it as a refuge.

I believe there are women all over the world who need to feel empowered to embrace a new, rewarding life after divorce. I realize your situation may be different from mine. My children are now older. My daughter is living on her own in another state, and my son is now a teenager. Yes, he needs guidance, but he is independent enough to give me the freedom I need to schedule clients and travel when it is necessary.

Perhaps you have younger kids who are more dependent on you, or maybe having your own business is not your desire. At the end of the day, the most important thing to consider is finding something that makes you feel joyous, happy, and purposeful. Creating a new and adventurous normal can be rewarding for you and your children. And by the way, if there *is* something you've been longing to do—such as start a business, write a book, take a dance class, or go back to school—give yourself permission to do it. Then go do it. If you're not sure how, then let's talk about how I can support you.

" If you don't
care for *you*,
who will? **"**

Chapter 6

To Thine Own Self Be True

I t may sound strange, but one of the gifts I received from my emotional and physical separation, and subsequent divorce was an intentional focus on self-care. It gave me an even broader perspective on well-being and forced me to really live inside the space of TruSynergy—mind, body, and spirit wellness. It was one of the things that sustained me during tough times. Not only did I learn the importance of personal wellness, but I also learned why many people struggle, divorce or not, with taking care of themselves.

I've had multiple conversations with clients, family, and friends over the last few years, and inevitably self-care has been a popular topic. Ironically enough, the common theme in just about every one of those conversations was that women didn't practice taking care of themselves as often as necessary. In fact, lack of self-care became a focal point of discussion during individual coaching and professional-development sessions because it was a barrier that stood in the way of enjoying many other areas of my clients' lives.

Let's Bust Some Myths

What I found is that many women struggle with practicing self-care because they've bought into three common myths that you, too, may recognize.

Myth #1: Self-care is selfish. The first myth is that women often feel it's selfish to do something for themselves. When I was growing up, I was taught to take care of family, to be a dependable worker, and to look out for friends. Yet I was never taught to take care of myself. I'm not just talking about brushing my teeth, showering, and grooming. I'm talking about a level of physical, emotional, and spiritual well-being that transcends outer appearance. This is not a knock on my upbringing because I come from a loving family. The topic of self-care was something my mom was never taught; at least, we never discussed it. Therefore, she didn't know to teach me how important it is.

Guilt and feelings of selfishness tend to set in when we decide to focus on something other than spouses, children, or work.

The truth, however, is that it's not selfish to take care of yourself. If you don't invest in yourself, you're potentially putting your health and wellness at risk by taking care of everything and everybody else, while ignoring yourself. If you've ever flown on an airplane, you know the safety exercise flight attendants go through that reminds passengers to put their own oxygen masks on first in the event of an emergency. This helps you to get the oxygen you need before helping someone else. Self-care is just like that. When you are intentional about taking care of yourself, it gives you the mental and physical energy to handle the other demands that come your way. This idea of self-care may not be easy to adopt after divorce, as I'm sure you've had a laundry list of things vying for your attention, including your spouse. However, it's imperative you learn to prioritize self-care, and I'll share some approaches for that later in the chapter.

I remember a point during my marriage when my husband and I were both in graduate school; we had a toddler and were both working full time. Then, I was not intentional with carving out time for me on a regular basis, so mind, body, and spirit wellness wasn't a central theme for me. We were too busy juggling work schedules, papers, and parenting. You may have fallen into the same trap. But toward the end of the marriage and throughout the divorce, me-time was essential. Workouts, walks alone in the park, reading, and prayer gave me a sense of peace and sanity. These were also great habits for stress relief.

If you've ever thought devoting time to yourself is selfish or something about which to feel guilty, I want to ask you two questions:

- If *you* don't care for *you*, who will?

- What is the impact on your well-being if you don't make yourself a priority?

Hopefully, honestly answering these questions will shift you to a new truth about selfishness and will prompt you to commit to new behaviors that focus on you.

Myth #2: We can do it all. We sometimes have the misguided notion that we can keep handling all our day-to-day responsibilities without taking time to pause and rest. I call this the Energizer Bunny syndrome because some of us think we can keep going and going on energy that will last forever. Part of the syndrome is a reluctance to ask for help, either because we're too stubborn, too embarrassed, or we can't accept that someone else may have a different approach than ours, even if it achieves the same desired result. You know how we can be sometimes. If we ourselves don't perform a task, then it won't be done correctly. This often leads to our running around as if we were chickens with our heads cut off—from one thing to the next. Rinse and repeat.

This applies to your regular daily schedule, so conversations with your partner and your children about divorce, family change, and meetings with attorneys or mediators add more time to already hectic schedules. Work, my business, transporting our daughter back and forth to college, and managing our son's sports schedule were important things to focus on while addressing the legal process of the divorce. I had to find that sacred me-time amidst all these activities. Morning walks at the park were, and continue to be, one of the best times for me, especially in warm weather. While writing this book, I've had many Facebook memories pop up with videos of me in the park; the dates on those posts coincide with the times that were challenging.

The reality is that we are not built to constantly be on the move, no matter how much we may tell ourselves we can, divorce or not. We need rest, and when we don't voluntarily take that rest, our bodies may have a not-so-funny way of forcing us to do so. Fatigue, tired muscles, headaches, elevated blood pressure, and inability to sleep can occur...and the list goes on. What happens when the gas tank of your car gets close to empty or your car needs maintenance? You stop for gas or take your car to the shop. Why? Because you know, if you don't, you won't get anywhere on an empty tank, and the car won't operate at its best performance without the care it needs; indeed, it may stop running altogether. We, in human form, are no different. So why would you give a car more attention than you'd give yourself?

We need to refuel daily before we've depleted ourselves of energy and joy. Going through divorce can certainly drain you physically and emotionally, so finding ways to nurture yourself as you go through it is essential. The bottom line is that we are wonderful creations, intricately designed to do amazing things, and when we rest, we regenerate and awaken with more energy and clarity of thought to be our best.

Myth #3: I don't have time. Does this sound familiar? "I don't have time to take care of myself," or "There are not enough hours in a day." I've certainly been guilty of misusing our most precious resource—time. I get it; you're juggling multiple tasks. Work, kids, business, aging parents, church, clubs, friends, and family may be tugging at you and claiming your attention. Throw in a divorce, and time really flies at warp speed!

The truth, however, is that we have more than enough time to do everything we *need* to do. I know it sounds totally unbelievable, but it's true. Here's why: There are twenty-four hours in a day. Is it possible that you could take one hour out of the day for yourself? For some, that may sound like a stretch, so let's explore further. There are sixty minutes in an hour. Breaking the hour into four quarter-hour increments helps to reframe time in such a way that seems much more manageable than sixty minutes. You may find it much easier to take fifteen minutes at a time than a whole hour at once. This means you're giving yourself time over the course of the day for self-care.

I can remember leaving quite a few mediation sessions with my eyes filled with tears. I used the travel time from the session to my next destination to get my cry out, pray, and take some deep breaths. Crying was a form of release for me because it meant that I was letting go of my emotions instead of keeping them bottled inside. Taking several deep inhales and exhales helped me settle my heart rate and gave my brain a chance to slow down from processing the events from the session. Focused breathing is one of the simplest and easiest ways to manage stress and practice self-care. The best part is that it only takes about thirty seconds to practice effective breathing, so that's one way to dispel the myth of not having enough time for self-care.

Strategies for daily self-care time management.

A fifteen- to twenty-minute car ride.

This can turn into a personal sanctuary, and those same breathing exercises can be a regular routine during times that are stressful and those that aren't. The change of scenery can make a world of difference; adding music and listening to something funny or inspiring can enhance the drive.

Eat a healthy meal.

Taking at least twenty minutes a day to eat lunch is also a great way to practice self-care. I don't mean working through lunch or shoving food down as you move from one thing to the next. I mean sitting down, chewing your food, and enjoying the flavors. I had a client who used to constantly eat at her desk while working. She expressed the need to focus more on self-care. During a few of our sessions, I challenged her to take time for lunch by stepping away from her desk, moving away from the computer, and eating. When she told me she actually followed through by moving to a different part of her office to eat, I was ecstatic! I would have preferred for her to walk away from her office altogether, but baby steps bring about change; that was one step in the right direction. When going through a divorce, stress may cause us to eat too much or not enough. Planning meals and taking the time to eat them will help you maintain your strength so that you have the clarity for decision-making and the stamina to manage the activities that require your attention.

A ten-minute shower.

Many of us bathe in the morning, at night, or both. This is another good place to practice deep breathing, light candles, and take in the sound of the running water. Water cleanses your body, but it is also relaxing, and it can help clear your thoughts. The more time you take to decompress, the more you open your mental space for creativity, to think about decisions that need to be made, and to better plan action steps that need to be taken, as they pertain to your divorce, life post-divorce, or life in general.

These are specific examples of how we can use short amounts of time for a quick reset. We can also take more extensive time for other activities, such as a day off, extended vacations, or spa time. It's not that we don't have time for self-care. We just have to rethink how we utilize time and then allocate it in such a way that it works *for* us, not against us.

Once I understood these three myths, it was much easier for me to be intentional with celebrating myself on a regular basis. In fact, the month of July became a symbol of personal liberation. My birthday is July 8, and my anniversary was July 9. I know you're wondering why in the world I'd get married the day after my birthday. The honest answer is that I have no clue! I literally just threw the date out there, probably after celebrating my birthday and thinking that would be a great way to keep having fun. In fact, my ex-husband used to call the back-to-back celebrations my "birthaversary," and we enjoyed it for quite a while. But there came a time when we weren't doing much celebrating, or we'd celebrate my birthday with the kids and ignore the anniversary. It became awkward for both of us; it was quite clear that there was no reason to celebrate anymore. So we didn't.

I was always grateful when my birthday came because, of course, another year of life is a blessing. However, I can remember how empty, lonely, and sad I felt on the day of our anniversary, knowing there'd be no acknowledgment of it. When that day came, it was as if there were an elephant in the room. By the calendar, it was significant, but saying, "Happy Anniversary," for formality's sake felt meaningless because it wasn't happy at all. I got tired of feeling this way, and I know my ex-husband did too. I decided that I would celebrate myself, not just on my birthday but for the whole month. I'd find something to do every day of the month to celebrate me, whether it was a walk, a dinner with family, or a vacation with girlfriends. It became a coping mechanism to help me get through. I also wanted my kids to see how important it was to practice self-care. It was a reminder for me to find joy during a difficult situation.

My monthlong birthday celebration paved the way for me to take more of a vested interest in my personal wellness; it encouraged me to make myself a priority. Whether you adopt a birthday-month approach or some other practice, don't wait to be celebrated. Find your own unique, magical, simple, exciting, fun, and joyous opportunities to enjoy being you. You're worth it, and you deserve it.

As a sidenote for the ladies who are not divorced, your commitment to celebrating yourself should not be an excuse for your spouse, or significant other, not to celebrate you. I'm just saying.

I fully support the increased calls for women to practice guilt-free self-care. We wear multiple hats every day (moms, daughters, sisters, friends, care-givers, employees, employers...and the list goes on). Add divorcée to the list, and the impact and responsi-bilities can be more intense. Each of these hats brings a set of responsibilities and decision-making that can be overwhelming, to the point that we may suffer from decision fatigue—as defined by ama-assn.org, this is a condition that occurs when there are so many decisions that need to be made that we lose our ability to do so effectively.

I'm guessing you don't need to imagine the stress and anxiety that comes with these responsibilities because you can probably identify with them first-hand. As women, we carry the unique blessing of being an asset in so many ways, but we also bear the burden of our capabilities because people often expect us to be that Energizer Bunny I referred to earlier. We fall victim to these expectations, consciously and unconsciously. Consciously, because we often feel compelled to prove our worth to others. Unconsciously, because we naturally go about the business of decision-making, problem-solving, prioritizing, transporting, loving, teaching, etc., with little thought. And, yes, it can weigh on us.

For Black women, the pressure is even more intense because there are spaces and industries that were not originally set up for Black women to succeed within them. *Forbes* conducted an interview with four successful Black women, and the comment from Luvvie Ajayi, *New York Times* bestselling author, resonated with me the most. She said, "The people I've spoken with feel the responsibility to not fail because we don't feel as if we can afford to fail. Our success is considered the exception, and our failure is considered the rule."

Read that again. Think about the added stress that comes along with being a woman, let alone a Black woman, feeling as though she must prove her success is *normal*.

I also heard an interview recently with Black female sports journalist Kimmi Chex. She stated how much pressure she puts on herself because she feels as if she can't make a mistake, which falls directly in line with Luvvie's comment on success and failure.

This is an all too common occurrence across many industries. Over my career, I've felt the need to present myself as a smart, educated woman so that people would see me as not just a Black woman, but also a smart person. However, I believe we tend to place unrealistic demands on ourselves, which can amp up our stress meter if we're not careful. This mental imprint can cause many women to ignore the emotional strain of divorce because they don't want it to impact their work, for fear of being seen as a failure.

Give *yourself* grace.

This highlights another area of personal wellness on which women should be laser focused—giving ourselves grace. It simply means we are humans and will make mistakes. When we do fall short, we should own it, take the lessons from the situation, and apply them in order to be better. Whether it's a failed marriage, a bad business decision, or being late for parent pickup at an after-school program, be gentle with yourself.

I had to remind myself of this several times, but in particular, when I was late picking my son up from weight lifting. At the time, he was in middle school, and he was going to his future high school for extra conditioning work. I dropped him off and went home to cook dinner. I knew he'd be starving by the time I picked him up at seven thirty, but when he called at seven fifteen to tell me weight lifting was over at seven, I panicked. All I could think about was that he had been sitting outside by himself—if anyone had seen him, they'd assume no one cared for him. See how quickly we can create stories and worry about what other people think? I turned off the stove and drove safely, but slightly fast at the same time, to pick him up. Luckily, the school was less than five minutes away, and he was safe. I apologized for being late, he teased me about it, and we laughed on the way home.

At the end of the day, I had to give myself grace, which is probably one of the simplest and most nurturing ways to love yourself. We won't always get it right. We'll have the wrong day, wrong time, or something that's not on the calendar at all. It happens. When we acknowledge this as fact and go easy on ourselves, it's a form of self-care.

In what ways do you need to give yourself grace? We are works in progress, not perfect people!

Consider therapy.

Therapy is another valuable form of self-care. I know this now, but it's not something I was taught growing up. Therapy wasn't part of our family history, and the reality is that I think we bought into the myth that many families believe, especially in the Black community—"What happens in this house stays in this house." Problems were handled within the family in order to keep family business from hitting the street. Unfortunately, women in some families suffered from stress, depression, mental and even physical abuse because of their silence.

Once during a lunch date with two dear friends, we talked about how much damage this code of silence causes for women. We shared how many of us have been afraid to talk about our struggles because we've been holding on to this myth while suffering in silence and carrying so much emotional baggage that we'd become weighed down by it.

Therapy also has carried the stigma that suggests one is weak or unstable if they choose this type of support. As I was brainstorming this chapter with my writing coach, Maggie, she shared how she didn't want to go to therapy while she was going through her divorce, even though she needed it. She didn't want to give her ex-husband any ammunition to suggest she was unfit to care for their son.

I would argue that going through therapy is just the opposite because it takes a strong woman to recognize her own limitations and boldly seek the help she needs. I believe the stigma around therapy is getting weaker the more we talk about the importance of mental health and self-care, especially in the post-COVID era with its impact on social issues.

Therapy has been instrumental for me, both as a part of marriage counseling and then as a practice I continued after my divorce. It allows me to work through my emotions in a safe, judgment-free space in which I can share freely, cry openly, and laugh heartily. Sometimes all in one session if I need to. My therapist was referred to me by a friend I trust. After the first session with her, I could tell that she was someone with whom I wanted to work and maintain the client relationship as long as I needed.

However, I've had friends who have changed therapists because the chemistry wasn't right, and they didn't feel the sessions were productive. If you consider therapy for yourself, be sure to find a practitioner with whom you have a good vibe, and don't be afraid to make a change if one doesn't serve you well. Changing therapists once or twice is okay, but more than that could hinder your growth because you'll have to rebuild relationships each time. Here are a few things to consider when looking for a therapist:

1. Check your employee benefits. Many employers have an Employee Assistance Program (EAP) that can provide you with covered options for therapy that may reduce your out-of-pocket expenses.

2. Ask friends and family whom you trust for referrals.

3. Research therapists in your area. Check their credentials, education, affiliations, and online reviews.

4. Create a top-three list of practitioners. Prepare a list of questions that are most important to you, and set up introductory meetings with each. First impressions mean a lot.

Therapy can be an outlet to manage going through divorce and day-to-day challenges; it can be a source of healing from deep-rooted trauma. Be open to it, especially if you've unsuccessfully tried other means on your own. Once you decide to say yes, be committed to the process and utilize it as often as you need. You'll thank yourself for it. Besides, therapy is not only an opportunity to help you heal and experience personal growth, but also a way to prepare you for having healthy relationships with family, friends, colleagues, or clients. Getting rid of your personal baggage makes it less likely that you'll carry it into the next relationship.

Decide when to share.

Personal advocacy is also a form of self-care. Not only does this mean making time and creating space to take care of yourself, but also it's about letting family, friends, and coworkers know when you need to do so. Remember to speak up for yourself when you're not feeling your best, emotionally or physically.

This is one thing I wish I had done differently, especially with work. I can remember leaving a therapy or mediation session, being a total wreck, wiping my tears, and going back to work as if all was well. I acted as if I were okay, even though I wasn't. I didn't want to tell anybody in my professional space, and even in my family, about the personal pain I was experiencing. Maybe I was wearing the *Super Woman* cape that many of us put on so often without knowing how or when to take it off.

I was working, going through a divorce, and trying to stay on top of my game. I managed, yes, but I also think there's a connection to another stigma that I now recognize was based on my work as a professional-development facilitator. Some leaders within organizations don't understand the importance of personal connections with their workforce and don't provide space for openness and vulnerability. Because of this, many women keep the cape on in meetings, on conference calls, and with clients—we keep moving. But the reality is that there's a risk that the quality and productivity of our work and our well-being will suffer.

You may not want to share your personal information with coworkers, especially if there is no closeness in your work relationships. However, you may need to share with the person to whom you report. Here is a statement you can use with your manager to advocate for yourself in the workplace when you're going through or healing from divorce:

> *I'm dealing with a personal family issue. I'm doing my best to manage work and home, but some days may be better than others. I may need support during this time.*

Depending on how comfortable you are sharing the information, you can insert "divorce," or whatever you're dealing with, in place of "family issue."

This gives your manager some insight in case there are changes in your work so that any change in performance will not be attributed to lack of skills or interest. It should also help your manager plan and utilize resources to provide the support you may need, whether it's time off, reassigning tasks, or collaborating with other team members to meet deliverables. This is a two-fold approach because it also requires managers to be open to communication and compassionate enough to provide the support needed. For some, this may require more personal advocacy, depending on the manager's leadership style, but stand up for yourself so that you get what you need. At the same time, recognize that, even though you should expect a certain level of support, your employer still has the right to require that you produce a reasonable amount of work, even through your trying times. Calling out every other day or constantly missing deadlines is probably not going to fare well. Stay in constant communication with your manager, and set realistic expectations about how you can be successful while going through your divorce.

If you own a business, and it's a solo practice, you're it! There's no manager for you to share your personal challenge with, unless you have a board of directors that provides oversight for your business. In which case, the advocacy statement mentioned above is still relevant to use with your board. Therapy and a strong support circle may be the best solutions to nurture your well-being and ensure your clients receive the best service from you.

I'm grateful because I get to share my lessons learned in this book, and it provides me with another strategy to share with clients in helping them find the fine line of harmony between maintaining professional integrity and personal wellness throughout the divorce process and beyond.

Self-care is a multilayered topic, and there are so many more aspects to it, including creating boundaries, curating space in your home or office, and practicing mindfulness, to name a few. This chapter only scratches the surface. I realize how common a challenge it is for people to invest in taking care of themselves, so every coaching program I offer includes a wellness component. As a certified meditation coach and facilitator, and a breath work instructor, I enjoy offering these simple yet effective practices to enhance the coaching experience. You can find more information at www.trusynergy.org.

Making yourself a priority may not be easy, especially if you have read this chapter and can identify yourself in any part of it. It first starts with a mindset shift that includes dispelling the myths I talked about earlier in the chapter. This will help you place greater emphasis on your personal value, which may be a crucial step for you after divorce. Once you do this, you'll begin to make self-care as necessary as breathing. Now is a good time to start.

" Those broken pieces are giving way to new births, new discoveries, and new possibilities. **"**

Chapter
7

Now What?

I was listening to an episode of Jada Pinkett Smith's Facebook show, *Red Table Talk*, on dating and relationships. She and a panel of four professional men were talking about relationships. One of the panelists, Devon Franklin, a film producer, author, and motivational speaker, said, "Every couple who says 'I do' never imagines the day when they don't." What a simple yet profound statement.

I couldn't agree more. We don't often prepare for the unexpected, so when we go through a divorce, it can leave us vulnerable and uncertain about what the next phase of life will look like. I never imagined being in my fifties and starting over. I remember I was driving home from the attorney's office with the question "Now what?" running through my mind. At that time, there was so much confusion, uncertainty, fear, anxiety, and sadness that it felt overwhelming to entertain the answer to that question.

Now, I find myself asking the same question, but with excitement, hope, anticipation, and, yes, some uncertainty. I still don't know if I'll get married again, or if I even want to. I haven't ruled it out, but I don't spend a whole lot of time thinking about it. Now, if Mr. Right comes along by the time you read this book, I'll be sure to tell you all about it in another forum!

In the meantime, I get to keep working on me, and that's both exciting and scary. It's exciting because I have the opportunity to really think about who I am, what I want, and how I want to show up for myself, for those I care about, and for the world I get to touch. But to do this, I have to keep focusing on inner personal work that often uncovers those little quirks, insecurities, and fears that cause me to fall short of the healthiest version of myself and prevent me from having healthy relationships. We all have things to work on that can make us better for ourselves and others.

My sister reminded me of a time when we were having a conversation, and I snapped back in a very defensive way to something she said. During the conversation, I was trying to get my point across, but when she brought it to my attention later that I was doing so, without really hearing her out. I had to acknowledge that she was right. I can count a ton of other times that I've responded the exact same way with her, in my marriage, and with others. Ouch!

Many of us—and that includes me—don't like to be called out on our own behavior, and we certainly don't like to admit that someone else is right about doing so. That's the scary part of the inner work because it will bring things to the surface that we'd much rather leave buried, especially when others see things about us that we don't recognize in ourselves. But I believe it's necessary that we all do this work. It can greatly improve the quality of our relationships with others and with ourselves. I've decided that this is what I will focus on going forward.

As I form new relationships with men, whether as friends or something more serious, I want to bring as little baggage as possible into the relationship. It's unhealthy and too much of a burden for me to carry the emotional strain from my divorce, or even from other areas of my past, into a new relationship; it's also unfair to those with whom I engage. This is true whether you're coming out of a marriage or a long- or short-term relationship. So often we move on to our next partner without taking the time to be still enough to reflect on what went wrong and what we have to do to prevent the same mistakes in our next relationship.

Stephan Labossiere, a speaker, relationship coach, and author, was another panelist on *Red Table Talk*. When asked about his perspective on meeting someone through a dating app, his response was clear and direct. He said to make sure you've done the work on yourself first, before getting into a relationship, or at the very least do the work in conjunction with your quest to find a new mate. After that, I started following Stephan on social media and listening to more of his conversations; it has been enlightening. As I continue self-discovery, I'm also intrigued to learn more about what men want, what they think, how they act, and the things that indicate alignment with what they want in a companion.

Personal inner work also gives us discernment into other people's unhealthy behavior, which can be signs of their unresolved issues. I haven't seen any major causes for concern on my journey to companionship, but here are some potential warning signs we should be aware of when interacting with a potential companion:

1. Makes comments, such as "I just can't live without you," or "I want to be with you all the time." Both can suggest an unhealthy dependence on you and the relationship for fulfillment and an unwillingness to honor time alone or with friends.

2. Expects an unrelenting level of support for their needs, but does not reciprocate that support for your ideas, dreams, and goals. This can demonstrate selfishness that may permeate multiple areas of the relationship.

3. Questions your whereabouts at all times in an accusatory manner. This behavior reflects insecurity that can become more intense and unsustainable over time.

4. Angers easily or is overly confrontational with you or others. This can create a toxic and unsafe relationship and potentially lead to emotional and physical harm.

A heightened sense of awareness of these behaviors is important at the beginning stages of relationship building, but it should be maintained throughout the relationship, especially if any of these types of behavior led to divorce in the first place. Such awareness can help us create the right boundaries to safeguard our well-being.

What I know for sure is that rarely does purpose and growth come without challenges. I wish it did, but unfortunately life doesn't work that way. Divorce can be tough, indeed, and my journey is a reminder of this fact. But it allows me to share what lies on the other side of divorce with women who can't see new possibilities for themselves. While the challenges can create the type of friction and chaos that make us feel as if we have no control over our emotions, or the situation itself, there are often hidden meanings and lessons to be learned during the challenges. It may take some time to fully realize the lessons. When we make a commitment to keep working on ourselves, the lessons will be clearer, appreciated, and ready to be used in meaningful ways to help others, if and when the opportunities present themselves.

There's so much to unpack when it comes to divorce, and each person's story and experience is different. There are nasty, knock-down, drag-out divorces with complicated financial and custody disputes. There are annulments after two people realize early on that the marriage was a mistake, and it would be better to end it before much time and emotion are invested. Then there are those less contentious divorces that are still difficult and emotional nonetheless, like mine. I've broken my experience into three phases that may help you as you're dealing with your own thoughts and feelings. I'll also recap some of the major points I've shared throughout, so no matter where you are in your process, you might find the answer to the "Now what?" question you may be asking yourself.

The first phase, or *Acknowledging,* is the period between separation and divorce. You and your spouse have come to an agreement that divorce is imminent. This, perhaps, is the most difficult phase because you're dealing with fluctuating emotions while working through the logistics for all the impending changes in your life and how they affect your children, finances, family, other relationships, and friendship circles. All this can be taxing.

The biggest lesson I learned during this phase is that communication—with each other and with kids if you have them—is crucial. Keeping your children informed about the process and how they will be impacted by the legal agreements is important. We fell short in this area. Be sure to have regular conversations with your spouse, or legal counsel, about the next steps and what responsibility each person has for items that need to be brought to closure. Don't wait months or years, as we did, to keep things moving, unless there are legal issues that have their own timelines. James and I tiptoed through this phase mainly because of our kids, which brings me to my second point.

Communicate early and often with your children. Don't assume that they can't handle the separation and divorce. We were so busy trying to protect our kids from what was going on that we didn't give them credit for being able to understand and be resilient. If you have children who are six and older, have the conversation in an age-appropriate way. The less you inform them along the way, the more information you'll have to share all at once, risking their emotional overload. That's not healthy for you, your spouse, or your kids.

The *Acknowledging* phase is also a good time to recognize that this is where the stages of loss (Denial/Isolation, Anger, Bargaining, Depression, and Acceptance) may begin to show up without warning. For this reason, it's important to surround yourself with support so that you have people to rely on when you experience these stages.

As I reflect, this is the phase in which I alienated myself. I didn't really want to share with my family and closest friends what was going on in my marriage, especially because we were the couple that many in the family admired. I should have let people in at this stage, rather than waiting until the *Thriving* stage, which I'll discuss later.

If you're in this phase, trying to figure out what to do next, think about in whom you can confide. It may be one person or two to three people, but keep your circle small so that you can maintain a safe and intimate space for conversation. You may only need your circle of support to provide a listening ear at times so you can get things off your chest and out of your head. Share your expectations with them before you meet for coffee or talk on the phone. This will give them clear direction on how you need them to support you. If you don't want them to give you advice or share their opinions, simply say, "I just need you to listen." This makes it clear for everyone up-front and helps relieve your inner circle from having to figure out on their own what you need.

During this phase, you may also tend to engage in negative self-talk, beating yourself up about all the things that have gone wrong in the marriage. I surely felt as if I were a failure several times, but I didn't want others to think the same, which is another reason I isolated myself in the beginning. But remember this takeaway: Just because your marriage failed, that does not mean you are a failure! I said it earlier, and it's worth repeating. I had to think and say this to myself over and over.

One suggestion is to write an affirmation on a sticky note, post it where you can see it every day, and read it aloud until you believe it. It can be as simple as, "My marriage has served its purpose, and now I get to find my purpose as I release it," or create your own affirmation that helps remove the stigma of defeat and motivates you to move forward.

There were times when I was angry because I thought about other people I knew who were able to reconcile and rebuild their marriages, yet we did not. I'm sure that somewhere in my prayers I tried to bargain with God, convincing Him of some promise I'd keep if He saved my marriage. I was even a little angry at God because at this phase, it was clear my marriage was not going to be saved, even though I prayed. God and I have since worked through this. I understand that even when we pray, the answer to the prayer may be better than what we asked for, take longer than we want, and work for a greater good than what we see in the moment.

Find your source, and lean into it. Also consider professional help to navigate through the *Acknowledging* phase and the other stages of loss. Therapy is one of the best investments I've made in my healing journey, and I still rely on it to continue my personal development.

The second phase is when the divorce is final—*Surviving*. I breathed a sigh of relief when James and I finished our final court proceeding, which was virtual due to COVID, and a little easier since we were not in the same physical space. The hearing felt so casual, as if we were just having a work meeting, rather than getting one step closer to ending our marriage.

However, I had mixed emotions when the final papers came in the mail. On one hand, I was relieved because we had finally gotten to the end point. Often during the process, I had told myself that I just wanted to be done with it and move on. Holding the papers in my hand and reading "Dissolution of Marriage" solidified it all. I remember thinking, *I survived the process.* The mediation sessions were over. The agreements were made. The kids, our family, and friends were aware. James had moved out of the house. On the other hand, I was sad because this was the final step.

In this phase, you may also find yourself surviving situations in which you and your ex must engage, especially where your children and a significant other are involved. I call these the by-products of divorce. James and I have a spot that's halfway between our houses; we meet there whenever my son's custodial arrangement switches. The first few times we met were awkward. I felt sad as my son got in his dad's car, and I drove away. Each of those times, I'd whisper to myself, "Okay, I got through that." *Surviving*.

Family traditions may change. Every Christmas Eve, James and our daughter went to the mall to do their last-minute shopping and enjoy daddy-daughter time. They loved the hustle and bustle. I'd stay home to prep Christmas dinner while they were gone. They'd come back to a clean kitchen and bake their cookies while I sat on the couch and enjoyed the sound of the mixer and the sweet smell of chocolate chip and oatmeal cookies. The first Christmas Eve after the divorce, the kids went to their dad and Michelle's for brunch. While they were gone, my sister and I relaxed on the couch and watched a movie. There were no cookies baking, and instead of that sweet aroma hitting my nose, a wave of emotion hit me as I realized how different that moment was. But I *survived* it.

The first soccer game that Michelle attended was a moment of survival because it was strange and a little uncomfortable. I just wanted to get through it. I'm sure she and James did too. Once we managed to do so, we headed to our cars and went our separate ways. I whispered yet again, "Okay, got through that." *Surviving.*

There are several key points to remember in this phase. First, rely on your faith source to help you get through conversations and interactions with your spouse or their companion. I can honestly say that I prayed before every instance I knew James, Michelle, and I would be in each other's company. I felt as if I needed a greater source of strength than what I could muster on my own. If you don't ascribe to a particular faith practice or belief, this is where you can rely on your circle of support that I mentioned earlier. Taking deep breaths before meeting in a social setting also helped me to relieve my body's response to feeling anxious. Pounding heartbeat. Tension in the temples. You know, the signs that let you know you're in stress mode.

Second, think of your children during the *Surviving* phase—really, all phases—and what example you want to set for them as you interact with their other parent and anyone that is important in their life. I wanted to show my kids how to be mature and respectful, even in the moments in which I was hurting, but I fell short sometimes. I shut down at times and felt a little sting when I knew the kids were spending time with James and Michelle. The kids were doing a great job with moving on and establishing a new family relationship. I never discouraged it. We never bickered or had harsh words with each other, but every family situation is different. If you need to have an intense adult conversation with a few choice words sprinkled in, do your best to have those discussions when the kids aren't around.

Last, as my therapist suggested, I looked at each moment of *surviving* as the next step in the healing process. She'd often tell me to consider every situation, thought, and emotion as its own milestone, to allow myself to *feel* through them, but to see each as an opportunity to get to the next best place. This reminds me of something I share with my clients about breaking complex problems or goals into manageable chunks. Doing so helps us to better process thoughts and ideas, take necessary actions, and, most of all, see results. Treat divorce the same way.

There is no timetable for the *Surviving* phase, and no one should define it for you or tell you to "just get over it." Healing is not linear, and everyone's journey is different. It would be nice to go through every stage smiling, laughing, and feeling good. There were moments when I felt that way. However, there will be moments when you're not okay and just doing the best you can to get over a thought or through a situation. I've had my share of those too. Actively using the tools I've shared, and others you discover on your own, will help you get to a place where you feel healthy, whole, and complete.

Maybe your divorce doesn't involve children at all, there is little to no interaction with your ex or a new companion, and you're only surviving through your own emotions. The circle of support, prayer, and professional help are still valuable tools to use as you strive toward the healthiest version of yourself after divorce.

The final stage is *Thriving*. This begins at the point that you've come to a level of acceptance that allows you to comfortably settle into the new family dynamic without needing deep breaths to manage anxious moments or telling yourself that you must "just get through" something. It's when you are truly free of the emotional strain found in the *Acknowledging* and *Surviving* phases. In the *Thriving* phase, you are at peace with family relationships and how they changed or stayed the same.

James and I may be divorced, but my sister and I, along with my ex-sisters-in-law, still have a good relationship. My sister still considers James her brother. Jessica has made it her mission to ensure we spend time together with our kids on Christmas Eve and during the summer. It's a new normal we've created that has taken the place of the Christmas Day dinners James and I used to host.

There are some areas of our lives in which I am still working on truly thriving. I was so used to our closeness. James and I were not only connected as husband and wife, but our siblings were more like blood relatives than simply being related by marriage. It feels strange to be excluded when certain events are taking place. Yes, this is tough for me, and I know I still have some work to do to thrive in this area.

There are many areas, however, in which we have thrived. Our children are settling into being part of a blended family. I, along with members of my family, were invited to the birthday celebration that James and Michelle hosted for our son. They included me in some of the planning and made it a point to have plant-based foods I enjoy. It was a considerate gesture that I appreciated, and it made me feel welcome in their home. It was a wonderful time. James, Michelle, and I enjoyed a glass of wine in my kitchen while waiting for our son to gather his things to return to his dad's. It was brief, but pleasant and cordial, and a moment in which we all felt relaxed. The conversation with Michelle about my invitation to their wedding was a *Thriving* moment.

While we were *Thriving* in many ways, I went back to *Surviving* on the day of the wedding. I knew it was fast approaching, but I was keeping it in a distant part of my mind until a week before the wedding. As the end of the week drew nearer, I was thinking, *It's almost here. Now what? Keep yourself together. You're okay.* After Michelle and I spoke and I decided not to attend the wedding, I was in a good place, or so I thought. I intentionally planned activities during the week before and on the day of the wedding to keep my mind occupied. Exercise. Meditation. Breathwork. Listening to music. Therapy. Manicure. Lunch. Dinner with my family.

In between each of these moments of joy and relaxation were quick spurts of heaviness, and I could hear the survival chant whispering in my ear, *I just want to get through this.* I had a mixed bag of emotions all over again. As I rode that roller coaster—feeling okay one minute,-not okay the next—I could hear my therapist's voice reminding me that this was a milestone. I wasn't distraught, wailing in desperation, and wondering how I was "gonna get my old man back," as Diana Ross screamed to Billy Dee Williams in the movie *Mahogany*. But it was a moment of reflection. This was the father of my children and once my husband. We'd loved and lost. We were moving on with separate lives.

Though I struggled more than I thought I would, and more than I care to admit, I got through the wedding day. I knew I made the right decision not to attend. I wished them well, but it was better to move through this milestone from afar.

There are some important points to focus on during the *Thriving* phase:

1. Celebrate the small wins when you achieve personal growth within yourself or with your ex-spouse and family.

2. It's okay to say you're not okay. Give yourself grace if you slip back into a moment of *Surviving* when you feel you've really moved on to *Thriving*.

3. Dealing with loss of any kind is not a straight line, and it's different for everyone. There may be simple things that trigger your emotions when you least expect it—a picture, a song, a date on the calendar, a wedding. Journal about how you feel and use number four below to help you handle your response to the triggers.

4. Keep handy your circle of support—close friends, family, or therapist.

These points can nurture you while *Surviving* and ensure that you stay focused while *Thriving*.

James, Michelle, the kids, and I have come a long way and are not where we were a few years ago. We will continue taking one step at a time as we keep building and defining our new family dynamic.

Marriage is sacred, and every couple who takes vows on their wedding day does so with the intent to commit for life—for richer, for poorer, in sickness, and in health, until death do you part. However, some marriages end. That's the reality of life. I never planned to be part of the divorce statistics, but I'm here. Now what?

Well, the best part is that I will continue the journey of self-discovery. I'm excited about whom I will find along the way—more about Ericka *and* who is out there to complement the happiness that I define for myself as I travel.

As I share my story with you, it is my goal to help you find strength, courage, and hope as you begin the process while going through your divorce or figuring out what's next when it's final. There will be ups and downs. Don't let anyone tell you how you should feel and for how long. It's okay to take the time you need to heal, but it's not okay to wallow in the pain and be a victim of your divorce. Be an active participant in the process of moving on so that you get to a healthy place of acceptance. Take what you can from what I've shared; then trust that you are more resilient than you think. When you surround yourself with the right support, you can make it through your situation, be happy, and find purpose. I will continue incorporating these messages in my services and on every platform available to me.

Though you may feel as if pieces of you died with the end of the marriage, those broken pieces are giving way to new births, new discoveries, and new possibilities. Embrace that part and do your best to enjoy it to the fullest.

> *Divorce isn't such a tragedy. A tragedy is staying in an unhappy marriage and teaching your children the wrong thing about love. Nobody ever died of divorce.*
>
> *~Jennifer Weiner*

E ricka Sallee is a speaker, self-help author, coach and owner of TruSynergy, LLC. Like the women reading this book, she wears multiple hats including mom, daughter, sister, and business owner, to name a few. She cherishes these roles but she also enjoys being a woman. Growing beyond lack of confidence and being bullied as a child, learning to embrace self-worth, and discovering new possibilities allows her to use her life as a canvas to inspire other women to create a masterpiece of their own.

She has a bachelor's degree in psychology from Frostburg State University and a master's degree in negotiation and conflict management from the University of Baltimore. In addition to her education and corporate experience, she has been coached and mentored by an array of leaders in the business and personal development industries.

Ericka established TruSynergy in 2010 as a personal coaching and professional development company that offers premier individual and group programs and services to its clients. TruSynergy helps women identify the barriers that stand in the way of their success and delivers the strategies to move them beyond those barriers to create the best version of themselves. If you're a woman longing to move beyond fear, self-doubt, the past, or even procrastination, to pursue change for healthier, purposeful and impactful living, then TruSynergy is your source.

Additionally, the Bold, Brilliant, Boss Leaders program is designed for women in leadership, or on a leadership path, who have a desire to improve self-awareness, build a personal brand as a confident and compassionate leader, and incorporate guilt-free daily self-care into busy schedules.

TruSynergy has also created a suite of professional development plans to support diversity, equity and inclusion, and other challenges in the workplace including effective communication, conflict resolution and team collaboration. These plans help organizations reshape their team culture to be dynamic, diverse and driven to focus on the human experience, as much as the bottom line.

There are two aspects that are incorporated into every coaching plan. The first is TruSynergy's signature approach, the IRP Method to Transformation, which is the process of Introspection (looking at where a client is in the present moment), Reflection (intentional consideration of past factors that contributed to present circumstances) and Projection (positively moving forward on the transformation journey). The second is a wellness component that TruSynergy believes is essential to transformation. When we invest time in our mental, emotional and physical well-being, we have more energy and capacity to make the meaningful changes we desire for ourselves. For this reason, self-care practices such as meditation and breathwork are included with coaching services, or as standalone options. It's transformation for the whole person!

TruSynergy's portfolio of corporate clients include Coca-Cola Consolidated, Maryland Public Television, Fulton Bank, Bowie State University, Summer Search (Philadelphia) and Maryland Department of Labor.

She has received many accolades and been instrumental in navigating her clients to powerful breakthroughs, which demonstrates her proven system for success. As a guest on multiple podcasts, delivering various keynote addresses and managing her diverse client base, she uses her voice to create transformation in the lives she gets to touch!

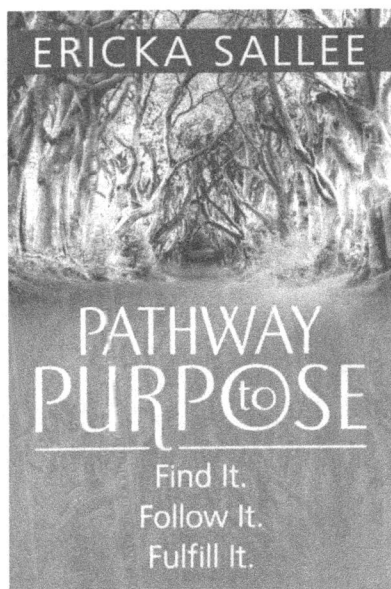

Pathway to Purpose: Find It. Follow It. Fulfill It.

ISBN Paperback: 978-1-71925-620-9

I published Pathway to Purpose: Find It. Follow It. Fulfill It. in 2018. When I started writing the book in 2007, it was initially intended to share my experience about starting my business. I got pregnant with my son and we bought a new house so I put a pause on writing but would later discover that the book would become much more than how to write a business plan. Years after my son was born, I went through a period of stagnation and wanted to uncover what was driving that feeling and more importantly, what I'd do once I figured it out. Pathway to Purpose highlights the journey to discovering how my life's events contributed to discovering revelations about my gifts, what made my heart sing and what I wanted to offer to the world. It may sound like cliché but I believe we all have a purpose that, if untapped, fuels and inspires us to be intentional with our actions.

The problem is that we sometimes ignore the warning signs (not happy at work, disappointed in relationships, regretting personal accomplishments) and we continue in our regular cycle of life, settling for unfulfillment. The good news is that this doesn't have to be you. If you're reading this and pondering the idea of creating something new and excited for your life, pay attention to the nudge. I did and I'm hoping you do too. You may be going through a transition and navigating your way to the next phase of your life. It just may be part of your purpose, or at the very least, help you begin figuring it out.

I share my journey to finding my purpose with the hope that you will also seek to discover what brings you joy and how that impacts the world you get to touch. Then pursue it with determination.

COACH · SPEAKER · AUTHOR

Let's Connect

Find out more about Ericka Sallee at the following links!

Official Website: www.trusynergy.org

Facebook | LinkedIn | YouTube: @ ErickaSallee

Instagram: @trusynergy_

www.ingramcontent.com/pod-product-compliance
Lightning Source LLC
Chambersburg PA
CBHW072045090426
42733CB00032B/2262